COOPERATIVE CLASSROOM TESTING

Larry G. Hanshaw

University Press of America,® Inc.
Lanham · Boulder · New York · Toronto · Oxford

Copyright © 2006 by
University Press of America,® Inc.
4501 Forbes Boulevard
Suite 200
Lanham, Maryland 20706
UPA Acquisitions Department (301) 459-3366

PO Box 317
Oxford
OX2 9RU, UK

All rights reserved
Printed in the United States of America
British Library Cataloging in Publication Information Available

Library of Congress Control Number: 2006922195
ISBN-13: 978-0-7618-3459-5 (paperback : alk. paper)
ISBN-10: 0-7618-3459-1 (paperback : alk. paper)

∞™ The paper used in this publication meets the minimum
requirements of American National Standard for Information
Sciences—Permanence of Paper for Printed Library Materials,
ANSI Z39.48—1984

Contents

	Preface and Overview	v
1	Utilizing Cooperative Learning Principles Within A Cooperative Testing Environment	1
	Research and Theoretical Perspectives on Cooperative Learning	7
	A Brief Review of Cooperative Testing Research	10
2	Cooperative Learning and Testing Principles At Work	23
	Examining the Instruction-Reinforcement-Evaluation Relationship	23
	Different Approaches To Using Cooperative Learning Principles	24
	The Cooperative Testing Environment Model	25
	A Closing Reflection on Cooperative Approaches To Student Achievement	33
3	Applying the Cooperative Testing Environment Model In the Classroom	35
	Comparison of Means From Composite Alone and Cooperative Group Test Scores (Question 1)	36
	Effect Size Estimates For Alone and Cooperative Testing Conditions (Question 2)	40
	The Cooperative Testing Condition and Intra-Group Position Changes (Question 3)	41
	Discussion of Intra-Group Improved Position Change Data	48
	Analysis of Intra-Group Improved Position Change Data	49

	Applications of Cooperative Testing in Science Classrooms	51
	A Science Teacher's Specialist Field Study	51
4	Cooperative Classroom Testing: Qualitative Considerations	53
	M.Ed. Portfolio Comments of Practicing Teachers and Graduate Students	54
	Closing Comments	58
Appendix		61
REFERENCES		65
INDEX		71

Preface and Overview

This book is written to promote the idea that learning is not limited to the sequence of instruction, reinforcement, and alone-oriented evaluation. Instead, learning also may be structured and extended to group testing episodes. Within such a structured testing environment, achievement may be maximized as students learn and interact face-to-face, exchange useful information and skills, and help one another to succeed even as testing occurs.

In the chapters that follow, readers unfamiliar with the idea of fostering learning during testing will be offered a brief review of research literature supporting cooperative learning and its relevance to the context of cooperative testing events. During such latter events, students' explanations to one another and their learned dependence upon one another create valuable sources of cognitive and social scaffolds (Woolfolk 1998). In turn, such helpful ways of doing and thinking contribute to an array of means by which students may better understand intellectual ideas and processes as interdependent persons within groups striving to reach a common goal (i.e., the highest test score possible).

Chapter 1: Utilizing Cooperative Learning Principles Within A Cooperative Testing Environment will focus on the use of cooperative learning principles within a cooperative testing environment. Both cooperative testing and cooperative learning will be defined within this context. Also presented in this chapter is an integrated discussion of certain attributes of cooperative learning found to be useful support structures for groups of students working cooperatively on regular teacher-made tests. This will be followed by a look at research perspectives and theory supporting cooperative learning and research involving cooperative testing..These definitions and discussions will give readers a foundation for understanding that cooperative learning has been primarily used as an instructional arrangement, while cooperative testing, as presented here, is a unique event that occurs after instruction but integrates many of the attributes of cooperative learning within a testing environment in order to maximize academic achievement. Chapter 1 will also present a brief discussion of cooperative testing research that covers a variety of investigations that many readers may find interesting. Moreover, many readers also may recall and find valuable the research relating to previously and currently used forms of "cooperative" efforts such as open book examinations, open notes allowed during examinations, and take home examinations. Because books and notes can only argue or defend ideas to a given degree, this section should probably be referred to as "assisted testing". Instead, alternatives forms of cooperative testing will be used to identify the investigations reviewed (i.e., in the Appendix). These studies represent interesting variations on the cooperative testing/learning theme. Such studies also may invite structural modifications that utilize cooperative learning principles in ways that might enhance test performance. A closing reflection on the use of cooperative testing will be provided as a reminder to readers that alone testing is not the only game in town when it comes to the appropriate use of valid ways to impact student achievement.

Chapter 2: Cooperative Learning and Testing At Work explores blending cooperative learning principles within the context of testing cooperatively. This is a unique aspect of what this book is about. One part of this blend will focus on the use of certain cooperative learning principles within the classroom (see, for example, Figure 1.1). The other aspect of this blend of ideas (i.e., Figure 2.2) will be centered on the roles of both teacher and students. The discussion of these roles will indicate how the Cooperative Testing Model works. For example, Figure 2.2 shows key aspects of cooperative learning principles at work in a cooperative testing environment. A discussion of the components of this model represents the ways in which the model was used in a variety of undergraduate and graduate classes from 1975-1998. The instruction-reinforcement-evaluation continuum will be discussed in order to help distinguish between efforts that focus on instruction as the starting point to improve student learning and achievement and efforts that focus on testing formats that also enhance student learning and achievement.

Chapter 3: Applying the Cooperative Testing Environment Model In the Classroom will be the center piece of this book. This chapter's quantitative focus will be a discussion of the statistical evaluation of mean test scores students achieved as they worked in both alone and cooperative conditions. The data analyzed in this chapter was drawn from experiments involving 321students who took regular classroom examinations in undergraduate and graduate classes over a period of three years (i.e., 1999 to 2001). Test results of students working alone and in groups (i.e, from this author's dissertation) also will be included. Chapter 3 will conclude with a summary of a field study conducted by a former graduate student who conducted research involving cooperative testing in a high school biology classroom. The results of this study indicate useful testing implications.

Chapter 4:Cooperative Classroom Testing: Qualitative Considerations will explore the qualitative side of cooperative testing and learning. This chapter contains a range of comments about cooperative testing from students who experienced cooperative testing either once or more than once due to the variety of classes I have taught over the years. Comments from experienced teachers and from those yet to hold school-related jobs full-time will also be discussed. Their comments may be insightful, since many of them indicated that they would be interested in trying this testing format in their own classrooms. Such comments may broaden our understandings of how teachers, teachers-to-be, and others who work in schools feel about a testing method that not only stresses academic achievement, but emphasizes, as well, certain social and emotional gains that can be derived from meaningful group work. References cited within the text of each chapter will be presented in a complete list of references at the end of this book. A list of authors and major topics within each chapter will be presented in the index. This should provide readers with an adequate number of sources to examine regarding the topics covered in this book.

Since 1975, and especially over the past several years, I have observed and tracked the alone and group performance of students and listened to their overwhelmingly positive comments as they worked cooperatively during testing.

This has been a very rewarding and informative research experience. I wish to thank my colleagues for their support and to give special praise to all of my students for their enthusiasm toward exploring what was for them an unfamiliar path to achievement.

Larry G. Hanshaw
The University of Mississippi, December, 2005

1
Utilizing Cooperative Learning Principles Within A Cooperative Testing Environment

Instruction, reinforcement, and evaluation are familiar components in the teaching process. At the beginning of this process, instructional methodologies may be in the form of Socratic questioning, inquiring-based teaching, discovery teaching, lecturing, or lecture-discussion. Of interest here, however, is the distinction that cooperative learning methodologies are used primarily during instruction whereas cooperative testing, of course, is a methodology used during evaluation. What if elements of the former (i.e., cooperative learning) were appropriately merged with elements of the latter (i.e., cooperative testing)? In this book, the nature of being "cooperative" during testing will not be treated differently from the nature of being cooperative when various instructional methodologies are discussed. Therefore, by carefully integrating cooperative learning principles into a structured cooperative testing environment, learning and student achievement may be enhanced (Webb 1997; Vygotsky 1978).

What, then, is cooperative learning and cooperative testing? Cooperative learning "is the instructional use of small groups so that students work together to maximize their own and each other's learning" (Johnson and Johnson 1999, 5). In previous research, cooperative testing was defined as "a variation [of competitive testing] that favors using cooperative interaction as a facilitating factor, but doing so during testing only" (Hanshaw 1982, 15).The research presented in this book is an extension of the "paired-cooperative condition" investigated earlier (Hanshaw 1982, 17) in that, currently, student groups: (1) are not limited to two person groups, and (2) learned about the "basics of cooperation" (Johnson and Johnson 1999, 75) through working together on various class assignments, taking group tests over the period of a semester, and benefitting from the repeated emphasis on and use of cooperative learning principles in my classroom and in others (see also Woolfolk's *Educational Psychology*, 7th ed., 1998, pp. 39-50). The specific elements of cooperative learning receiving the most emphasis in relation to group testing are shown in Figure 1.1.

My first exposure to the concept of cooperative testing occurred in 1975 during the years of study needed to complete a Ph.D. in science education at the University of Southern Mississippi in Hattiesburg. It became clear to me early on that much of what happens in real world work places such as schools, hospitals, and various industrial settings is the result of cooperative efforts of individuals as well as groups (Ledlow 1999).Then, and now, the question of whether two heads are better than

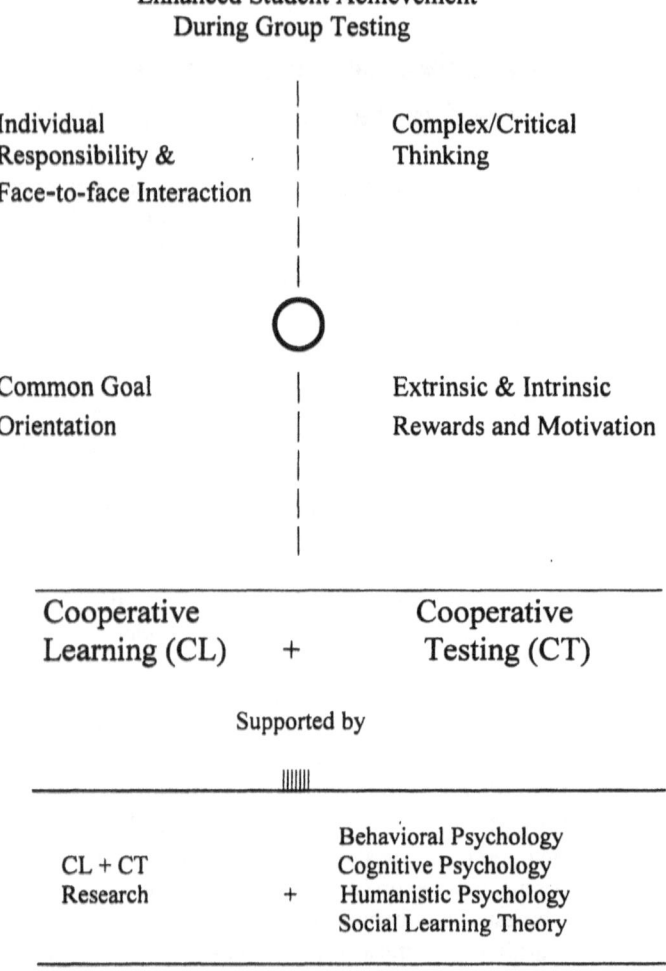

Fig. 1.1 Cooperative Learning Strengthens Cooperative Testing

one in an academic setting has remained an intriguing problem deserving further research. In this book, this question is approached from the evaluation side of what happens in classrooms. That is, as in real life, why not have students learn about and use the principles of cooperative learning within a cooperative testing environment? Other researchers (Johnson and Johnson 1994; 1999; Slavin 1995; and Armstrong and Savage1990) have published numerous works explaining their perspectives on the subject of cooperative learning as an instructional methodology. The information and explanations in their books and articles have been used in my classroom as frameworks to address and clarify many of the complexities that surround group and individualistic efforts in an intellectual setting. However, my interest in cooperative testing has over the years focused on acquainting students with the principles of cooperative learning as a spring board for how students might maximize their performance during group testing.

For example, the information in Figure 1.1 on page 2 summarizes the particular elements of cooperative learning that have proven to be the most essential components applicable to the particular cooperative testing methodology employed within this author's classes over the years. Each of the four factors shown in Figure 1.1 was integrated into class discussions of regular course content material to help students understand the body of literature supporting cooperative learning and its relationship to cooperative testing. Students were told about these factors during the initial course meeting and as the course progressed. Students then voted on whether they wanted to experience cooperative testing as part of the overall evaluation within a course. This was important, since none of my first-time students had ever participated in group testing, but were already somewhat familiar with the principles of cooperative learning. Their prior knowledge of cooperative learning principles and discussions of the benefits of cooperative learning more easily enabled me to help students make relevant connections between cooperative testing and cooperative learning (i.e., CT and CL, respectively, in Figure 1.1).

Within the structure of our undergraduate programs, students also learned about cooperative learning as an effective instructional methodology. They learned about face-to-face interaction,(2)positive interdependence,(3)individual responsibility, the necessity of developing (4) interpersonal and small group skills (Johnson and Johnson 1975; Johnson, Johnson, Holubec, and Roy 1984; Armstrong and Savage 1990; 1998) and (5) the facilitation of group processing by the teacher and on the part of group members (Johnson and Johnson 1994).

In the top half of Figure 1.1 are four factors selected from those discussed by Johnson and Johnson (1999).The information in the bottom half indicates the research literature's broad support of both cooperative testing and cooperative learning in relation to student achievement. The bottom half of Figure 1.1 shows the fields of psychology that provide theoretical explanations for learning that occurs in groups and individuals. The bottom half will be dealt with in more detail in Chapter 2. Readers, however, should review for themselves the research literature's support of both cooperative testing and cooperative learning.

Relative to the factors in the top half of Figure 1.1, the circle shown is symbolic of a steering wheel with four spokes (i.e., individual responsibility and face-to-face interaction, complex/critical thinking, common goal orientation, and motivation). These are critical elements needed to power and control the direction of a ship aboard which all students in a group are passengers. Hence, success as a group *during testing* is dependent upon how "all hands on board" pitch in to ensure that the group reaches its intended destination (i.e., the group achieves the highest grade possible as a result of helping one another during a test). This was presented as interdependence and common goal orientation. Along the way, as I have so often stated to groups, it is beneficial to all if everyone has a voice in decision making (i.e., interaction). That is, decision-making helps individuals achieve ownership in the potential outcome as groups work toward a common goal. Maximum individual efforts under these interactive conditions could enable group members to respect each other and value contributions each would make towards group success (i.e., common goal orientation). However, after input or the sharing of information from everyone ends, groups were told to let the chips fall where they may regarding the final decision affecting what an individual records on his or her answer sheet (i.e., individual accountability and responsibility). This metaphoric style of discussing each of the "four spokes" shown in Figure 1.1 helped students to internalize their roles within cooperative groups as others (Smith and Waller 2004; Ledlow 1999) have also found helpful. The group's expectation, therefore, was that academic achievement might be enhanced for all group members.

Individual Responsibility/Accountability

Students in cooperative testing groups were asked to prepare for scheduled tests with themselves and others in mind. This stipulation stressed the importance of maintaining individual responsibility for course material even though others in the same group would be similarly preparing themselves. One's inability to contribute to discussions on group tests was a sure way to expose not having studied. Being told ahead of time, groups could use such observations of individual group members in order to rid themselves of dead weight. On this particular point, it is important for teachers in college and lower level classes to warn individuals before consigning non-contributors to taking their exams alone. Group members armed with this knowledge knew that one strike would not trigger such a consequence. Only two individuals suffered this fate from 1999 to 2001. Over the years, in undergraduate and graduate classes, I have noticed that students strongly desire to minimize what I have called being a "gold brick"; a term from my military experience that refers to individuals that either do not carry their own weight or who fail to display esprit de corps. Thus, the idea of an individual expecting a free ride almost always gave way to individuals preferring to be stakeholders in a group's success. Since cooperative testing was instituted back in 1999, involving classes that provided the most recent data for this book, all students were asked to provide phone numbers and e-mail addresses to one another as a way of knowing when group meetings would be held or how a member could be reached in case of an unforeseen emergency. Students also had the responsibility of informing the instructor concerning any absence(s) from class. Announcements of such information would take place during class and this seemed to preserve an individual's accountability as a team player among group members and the class as a whole. Most groups met at least once to study together prior to either an alone or a group test while other groups met after class to discuss and to align notes taken during class. Students within the same group managed these opportunities to get to know one another better. This fostered a dependence upon others' skills and helped to develop the level of confidence in each other's abilities that group members displayed (i.e., individuals showed they were willing to put in the time to prepare themselves and to assist group members in similar ways). I reminded my classes that this kind of behavior would likely be a factor in how well individuals within a group would jell socially and perform as a whole during testing. Thus, the interactive and face-to-face conditions typical of study groups became part of the preparation for success on both alone and group tests. Evidence of how students assisted one another prior to and during examinations is dealt with in more detail in the student comments presented in Chapter 4.

Complex/Critical Thinking

In a lecture-discussion based classroom, it is beneficial to students trying to learn course content if discussions during lectures allow students to connect their experiences to and to voice thoughts regarding the multiple views found in textbooks and those expressed by the teacher. Teachers that encourage students to express their own thoughts and, conversely, to discuss the thinking of others, create an atmosphere in classrooms that facilitates the learning of course content at higher levels of thinking (McKeachie 1988). Moreover, the use of good teacher questioning practices allows students' faulty reasoning to be exposed. Good questioning further stimulates students to weigh, to criticize, and to synthesize new points of view with attention given to available evidence supporting a given view, regardless of the personal values they may hold toward ideas being discussed (Ruggiero 1988). Fostering learning opportunities in this context (Kauchak and Eggen 2005) often enables students to grow into persons that will make good judgments; judgments that are based upon reliable information. Such a process is a way of enabling students to become critical thinkers (Kauchak and Eggen 2005,402). Students working collaboratively learn from one another as they engage in resolving different answers to test questions (Piaget 1980). This sharpens their ability to make better judgments as they make use of their own thinking strategies and those they adopt or manipulate from others (Armstrong and Savage 1998; Johnson and Johnson 1999; Jacobs 2000; Wittrock 1974).On some occasions students asked for clarification on some questions and even tried to involve the instructor as some sort of referee to help decide who was right! This, of course, was not my responsibility, if the clarity of the question itself was not the issue. With only themselves as resources, students learned to sort out their own decision-making differences and not to expect the instructor's assistance.

Common Goal Orientation

Few teachers have not experienced questions from students regarding how their grade in a course would be determined. For all of my students, having the chance to work in groups *on a test* was new territory in that none of them had ever done this sort of thing before and the chance to do so created excitement and new positive expectations. For example, the difficulty of some courses (i.e., advanced curriculum, theory, and practice and educational research, among others) made many students admit that they initially would have settled for a passing grade and not necessarily the highest grade possible. Given a chance to work in groups and to apply the principles of cooperative learning, however, opened the door to greater expectations because students sensed the many benefits of a team effort inherent in reaching a common goal (i.e., a higher grade than expected). Perhaps the shift toward supporting a common goal was due to the novelty of cooperative group testing or that many students formerly were members of debate teams, football or basket-ball teams, concert bands, or other activities where the outcome of a group effort was not due to one individual effort alone. Relating my own successful experiences to such group involvements, however, lent credibility to what could happen in a group testing environment. Thus, the likelihood that the highest grade possible *could be* attained if everyone helped everyone else understand the material covered in a course from test to test became an operational reality. Moreover, students sensed that risk in a course could be reduced through a common effort to achieve the highest score possible (i.e., I will do what I can to help the group and they will be there for me). This was a strongly motivating force (Armstrong and Savage 1998) within groups engaged in cooperative testing. Students also expressed that group testing affords a reduction in stress. That is, the anxiety of possibly sinking alone was replaced by the lesser anxiety state of possibly going up together. As some stu-dents have put it: "working by myself, I felt I would not have done as well; but just having someone else contribute their ideas during testing made taking the test easier".

Extrinsic and Intrinsic Rewards and Motivation

Students preparing to become teachers share many micro-opportunities to teach even before they enter the classroom as paid professionals. In a group testing environment, students utilize what they have learned about cooperatively working with others (i.e., individual and group responsibility, face-to-face interaction, positive interdependence, common goal orientation, and group processing) to achieve a common goal (i.e., the highest course grade possible). In the act of doing so, they teach one another; the same act they will perform as individuals and as members of, perhaps, a team of teachers. Consider, for example, a second grade teacher who learns from a team member how to best teach reading using the whole language approach instead of the phonics approach with which she or he may be more familiar.

Or, consider a novice high school chemistry teacher that learns from a more experienced chemistry teacher how to best help students learn how to solve tricky oxidation-reduction reactions. In both of these instances, group interaction gets converted into an individual act. From a motivational aspect, both teachers in the above examples could be motivated to become better professionals on their jobs and are, therefore, beneficiaries of both the extrinsic rewards (i.e., "rewards that come from outside oneself" (Kauchak and Eggen 2005, 8) and the intrinsic rewards of teaching (i.e.,"rewards that come from within oneself and are personally satisfying for emotional or intellectual reasons" (Kauchak and Eggen 2005, 6)).Both types of reward are interactive and common to working in educational environments. These sorts of interactions are not limited to K-12 environments, of course, since the same scenarios can be, and are, typical of interactive relationships involving, simultaneously, intrinsic and extrinsic rewards (see Kauchak and Eggen 2005, 9) and their relationships to motivation in higher education settings (see, especially, Pintrich 1990).Thus, teacher education students, who work in a cooperative testing environment, are likely to experience similar dynamics of learning, teaching, and motivation like others who work in the small social groups found in the real-world environment of schools.

Research and Theoretical Perspectives on Cooperative Learning

Slavin, in *Cooperative Learning,*2nd edition, described six principal characteristics of cooperative learning: (1) Group Goals, (2) Individual Accountability, (3) Equal Opportunities for Success, (4) Team Competition, (5) Task Specialization, and (6)Adaptation to Individual Needs. These characteristics are elements of cooperative learning for groups that work together toward a common goal within a structured cooperative learning environment. For more specifics on the discussion of these elements by Slavin, see *Cooperative Learning*, 1995, pp. 4-13. Additionally, Slavin discusses the connection between cooperative learning and certain theories of learning (i.e., motivational, cognitive elaboration, and developmental). The views he expresses relative to cooperative goals helps to explain why cooperative learning is superior to traditional learning practices found in schools. Slavin indicates, for example, that "clearly cooperative goals create proacademic norms among students, and proacademic norms have important effects on student achievement"(1995, 17).From this perspective, when students are given an opportunity to work together and to apply psychological principles that support working together, students do so in ways that carry-over and influence their behavior and achievement in both instructional (see Slavin 1995, pp. 23-24) and test-taking environments (Zimbrano et al 2003, p. 101).This latter conclusion is further supported by Slavin's summary of research studies that examined the effects of cooperative learning on achievement. He reported results of numerous studies (his among them) involving cooperative learning methods versus non-cooperative methods as a control. Also reported were effect sizes (for example, see Tables 2-1 to 2-8, pp. 22-24).In terms of achievement outcomes, Slavin states that "overall, the effects of cooperative learning are clearly positive. Sixty-three (64%) of the ninety nine experimental-control comparisons significantly favored cooperative learning. Only five (5%) significantly favored control groups. However, it is clear from looking across the tables that achievement effects vary widely, depending on methods and many other factors" (1995, 21).The effect size of +.26 he reported, im-plies that there is strong evidence for the latitude teachers have in the choice of cooperative learning methods that can be used. Lastly, in Table 2-10, p. 41, Slavin provides some guidance for results of cooperative studies that only involved a selected use of characteristics related to cooperative learning instructional methods. For example, in 52 studies involving Group Goals and Individual Accountability only, the effect size was +.32; for nine studies involving only Group Goals, the effect size was +.07; for 12 studies involving Individual Accountability (Task Specialization), the effect size was +.07; and for four studies involving No Group Goals or Individual Accountability, the effect size was +.16 (Slavin 1995, 41).Other leading researchers also have examined underlying theories, conditions, and rationales that explain the positive and negative interactive effects of cooperative learning outcomes versus other goal structures (Johnson and Johnson 1999). For example, throughout their book, *Learning Together and Alone: Cooperative, Competitive, and Individualistic Learning*, the Johnsons promote the ideas of (a) integrating goal structures into lessons taught in schools and (b) enabling students to know when to compete and when to work together and alone (see Johnson and Johnson 1999, x).They also list and discuss (1) positive interdependence, (2) face-to-face promotive interaction, (3) individual and group accountability, (4) appropriate use of social skills, and (5) group processing as the "basic components of effective cooperative efforts" (Johnson and Johnson 1999, 75). Moreover, they also provide (i.e., in Appendix A, pp.183-218): (1) an informative and excellent summary connecting schools of thought in the field of psychology to cooperative learning and group behavior, (2) a history of cooperative learning, and (3) a summary of research that "directly compares the relative effects of competitive, individualistic, and cooperative efforts" (Johnson and Johnson 1999,184-218). Throughout the book the authors provide a wealth of documentation that is both theoretical and practical research that supports the use of various cooperative learning arrangements along with traditional individualistic opportunities to learn and to achieve. For example, in reference to work done in 1989, the authors point out that their meta-analysis of more than 375 studies found that "the average student cooperating performed at about two-thirds of a standard deviation above the average student learning within a competitive (effect size = 0.67) or individualistic situation (effect size = 0.64). When only high-quality studies were included in the analysis, the effect sizes were 0.88 and 0.61, respectively. Cooperative learning, furthermore, resulted in more higher-level reasoning, more frequent generation of new ideas and solutions (i.e., process gain), and greater transfer of what is learned from one situation to another (i.e., group to individual transfer) than did competitive or individualistic learning" (Johnson and Johnson 1999, 202-203).In *Cooperative Learning in the Thinking Classroom: Research and Theoretical Perspectives*, Jacobs (2000), addressed four questions that, in turn, provide helpful insights into the connections between thinking and cooperative learning. These insights also provide understandings about the dynamics of what occurs within cooperatively testing groups. Specifically, he addressed questions related to (1) what makes cooperative learning distinctive from just groups that work together, (2) research about the effectiveness of cooperative learning in promoting thinking, (3) the conditions in cooperative learning that help promote thinking, and (4) the theoretical perspectives that support the "cooperation-thinking" link (Jacobs 2000, 1).

With regard to question (1), the author indicated that cooperative learning is very different from groups that just work together in that cooperative learning has "carefully prepared, planned, and monitored"group work (Jacobs 2000, 1).This includes the essential elements of perceived positive interdependence, face-to-face promotive interaction, individual accountability for one's own learning, as well as the learning of other group members; the teaching of collaborative skills, and how information can be processed interactively by groups in ways that improve group members (Jacobs 2000).The second question explored the promotion of thinking in the context of cooperative learning that should involve: (1) observing "how students *produce* knowledge rather than how they merely *reproduce* knowledge" while using tasks that "extend, refine, and use knowledge in meaningful ways" (Jacobs 2000, 3).In the third question, research supporting cooperative learning and thinking was presented in two categories (i.e., summarized in Tables 1 and 2, respectively).In the first category, six studies showed "cooperative learning to be "more effective" in promoting thinking on higher level tasks" than other methods (Jacobs, 2000,4-6); and in the second category, four studies found that "cooperative learning was "no more effective" in promoting thinking (Jacobs 2000, 6-7).The fourth question addressed theoretical perspectives supporting the connection between thinking and cooperation. These studies drew upon theoretical views in the fields of social, developmental, cognitive, and humanistic psychology. Motivational and multiple intelligence theories were also included. The views of specific theorists from each field of psychology and examples of cooperative methods that operationalized these understandings were also offered. The overall conclusion Jacobs reached regarding the four questions above was that "cooperative learning can support an environment in which students feel encouraged to take part in higher order thinking. However, more work needs to be done on how to best to build [sic] the cooperative learning-thinking link" (2000, 20).For a full review of the above discussion and other studies cited, as well as effect sizes noted (see Jacobs 2000, pp.1-20).

The research cited through out this chapter is evidence supporting the position that cooperative learning principles can be effectively integrated within a sound cooperative learning instructional methodology. Testing methods that utilize the same psychological principles effectively becomes cooperative learning operationalized within a testing environment (Hanshaw 1976; 1982; Meinster and Rose 1993; Felder and Brent 1994; Zimbardo, Butler, and Wolfe 2003).

A Brief Review of Cooperative Testing Research

Table 1.1 presents a summary of key features of several college-level cooperative testing studies and other publications (i.e., published proceedings). Some studies or publications date back to the early 1930's, while others are more recent. The selected studies and publications included in Table 1.1, however, are those that: (1) dealt with test achievement as a major outcome along with other achievement-related variables (i.e., social or psychological) as study objectives for students in a college class environment and (2) may or may not have involved cooperative learning principles as a focus, except where expressly stated in this review. Readers may wish to examine the information presented in these studies for details that go beyond the scope here of examining settings where cooperative testing played either a major or a minor role within these investigations.

Obviously, time has changed the attention paid to statistical treatment of data, variables investigated, and the many principles and theories more widely known and accepted now than in earlier times. Nevertheless, much can be gained conceptually by examining previous research efforts, since any methodology can, theoretically, be improved or, at least, can serve as fertile soil for future and better research efforts.

Table 1.1 College-level Cooperative Testing Research

Author(s)	Design	Results\Conclusion
Berry and Leonard (1974)	Affects of pairing on test performance; 30 students in two groups rotated as control groups between two tests.	On two tests paired groups produced significantly higher means than the singles' group.
Bowen and Phelps (1997)	Two sections of first semester general chemistry and engineering majors course involving one treatment and one control group in each section; 85 students total. Students worked together in self-selected treatment groups on questions.	Treatment students outperformed control students on four exams covering common items and demonstration-based assessment items.
Dougherty, Bowen, Berger, Rees, Mellon, and Pulliam (1995)	Students in three general chemistry sections were exposed to three different modes of instruction: Lecture and no enhanced (e-mail or paper mail) communication, structured cooperative learning with enhanced communication (i.e., course credit offered for communication by e-mail), and unstructured cooperative learning with enhanced (course credit) communication by paper mail. Students in the structured cooperative section had group quizzes and group homework, and were required to belong to a study group. The unstructured cooperative group was encouraged to form optional informal groups.	Based upon common questions on the final exam, students in the two cooperative groups got 58% and 60% of the items correct (structured and unstructured groups, respectively). The control group got 55% of the common items correct. There was no significant difference between the percent of items correct for the two cooperative groups. It was concluded that performance and retention can be improved by a structured cooperative setting and communication.

Table 1.1 (Continued)

Author(s)	Design	Results\Conclusion
Felder and Brent (1994)	Three to four students assigned by instructor for semester with only one A student among the four having previously received A's in specified mathematics and physics courses. Individual roles rotated within groups. Five 200 300, and 400 level classes in chemistry used involving 118 students. In-class and homework assignments used where teams set solutions individually and worked final solutions as a team.	Using one class as a case study, groups earned grades more toward higher end than groups taught in a non-cooperative setting.
Furuhata (1965)	Two four-member teams of 266 cooperative and 257 competitive students used to study productivity (achievement), cohesiveness, and group participation relative to a puzzle and a discussion problem.	Cooperative groups earned higher scores on all variables than competitive group.
Hall, Sidio-Hall, and Saling (1996)	Ninety-five students divided into 3 groups studied a lengthy word passage to test their sensory processes (individuals studied knowledge maps, pairs studied passage using scripted learning, and a third group studied in a way of their choice). After two days, students completed a free recall test on transfer. Two days later studied a second transfer passage using a method of their choice and completed a second free recall test on another transfer passage.	Students in scripted learning groups recalled more information on both tests than the other two groups. The scripted cooperative learning method was very effective for transfer but the knowledge map method was not effective for initial learning.

Table 1.1 (Continued)

Author(s)	Design	Results\Conclusion
Hall, Mancini, and Hall (1996)	Two person groups in a college psychology class used scripted learning to study class materials using both cooperative learning and cooperative testing formats. Test were completed immediately following studying and two days later.	Immediate retention results were better using cooperative learning; cooperative testing strategy worked best for long term retention; the latter results, however, pertained to delayed recall only.
Hancock (2004)	Using lesson plans designed around cooperative learning principles of Johnson and Johnson (1999), 52 participants in two nearly equal sections of a research methods course, used cooperative learning principles within assigned groups of three or four students. Peer orientation effects on achievement and motivation studied for a college population.	Students with high peer orientation scored higher on achievement test after 15 weeks of course; results were not significant. Graduate student values toward learning over social interaction and discussion dominance rival effects of peer orientation on achievement.
Hanshaw (1982)	Forty-six students in three college science classes were randomly assigned to two person groups that took three teacher-made exams. Two classes had seven pairs each and a third had nine pairs. Students relied on each other's math skills, content knowledge, and freely communicated to solve problems. Each half of a test was alternately in the group or the alone	Students working in pairs produced significantly higher mean composite test scores in all three classes. Also, post-study calculations of original published data found effect sizes of .55σ for the

Table 1.1 (Continued)

Author(s)	Design	Results\Conclusion
	condition. Answers were recorded by student pairs on separate answer sheets. GPA's used to match team pairs that worked together during the entire study.	biological science class, and .73σ and .60σ for the two physical science classes.
Husband (1940)	Forty pairs and forty individuals in a psychology class were compared on the basis of time consumed to solve a word puzzle, a jigsaw puzzle, and five arithmetic problems. Some participants were friends and others strangers.	Pairs did better on code and jigsaw tests, but no differently than individuals on math problems. Friends did better than strangers.
Kaufman, Felder, and Fuller (2000)	A peer rating system was used to determine the performance of cooperative learning teams that completed homework assignments in two second-year chemical engineering courses. Individual project grades and team rating factor determined final grade. Assigned roles rotated within teams across assignments. 191 students stayed in both courses (121 in CHE 205 and 70 in CHE 225).	Males earned higher normalized final grades than females did in both courses. Rating system use judged to be effective and outweighs problems that sometimes occur.
Lambiotte, Dansereau, Rocklin, Fletcher, Hythecker, Larson, and O'Donnell (1987)	Seventy-four undergraduate psychology students participated in a study of the impact of cooperative interactions during studying and test taking. Dyads learned together and were tested together and alone while individuals learned alone and were tested alone and together. Free recall tests measured transfer of cooperative test-taking training to individual study and test taking.	Strategies based on cooperative study and training produced better performance and transfer results in relation to recall accuracy.

Table 1.1 (Continued)

Author(s)	Design	Results\Conclusion
Ledlow (1999)	Though not a study on specific group testing arrangements, the information provided by the author is informative in terms of studies and suggestions from research on the positive and negative aspects of group grading which represents important implications for users of group testing arrangements.	Give grades and rewards that respect how they were produced. Avoid grading on the curve.
Meinster and Rose (1993)	Students in three developmental psychology classes participated in a study to determine whether a cooperative testing or individual testing format would reduce anxiety and produce better performance. Two sections used cooperative testing (i.e., 27 students and 15 students); the third class was used for comparison purposes. Initially, students chose their partners, then rotated to new ones; participation was by choice. Students had their own answer sheets. Items on the exam asked students to rate their anxiety levels and to indicate a preference for an exam mode. Four 50 item multiple choice tests used.	Cooperative testing classes had higher mean scores than the other testing mode; however, results were not uniform within the cooperative testing classes. No anxiety differences were found, but students did express a choice for the cooperative testing format. However, with repeated exposure, anxiety tended to decrease.
Monk-Turner and Payne (2005)	Students in an upper level research methods class were used to investigate how students perceived group work after completing a semester long project. 145 students participated in the study.	Data from the study indicated that small groups worked together more effectively than larger ones. Also, students with high grade averages expressed more concerns about group work than others.

Table 1.1 (Continued)

Author(s)	Design	Results\Conclusion
		Students that were less positive about group work also had time constraints competing with the demands of group work.
Orbell, Van de Kragt, and Dawes (1988)	Two experiments were conducted involving a social dilemma game to determine the influence of a period of discussion among group members on cooperation.	The first part of the study indicated that discussion alone does not promote cooperation. When members of a group promise to cooperate is an important part of explaining the influence of discussion on cooperation. A second part of the study showed that rates of cooperation greatly increased only when all group members promised to cooperate.
Reid, Palmer, Whitlock, and Jones (1973)	Two separate experiments compared the performance of students in a beginning college algebra course using computer-assisted instruction. eighty-one pairs of randomly assigned students were pre- and post-tested and their achievement scores were compared to those of thirty pairs of females and forty-six pairs of males from an earlier study.	The comparison of the two groups indicated that the pre- and post-test mean scores of individuals in the paired groups was always greater than the individual mean scores of those who worked alone. The authors also stated that more efficient

Table 1.1 (Continued)

Author(s)	Design	Results\Conclusion
		learning may be the result of students assisting each other.
Skidmore and Aagaard (2004)	Researchers conducted an experiment that allowed students to employ active engagement with course materials in four conditions: independent, cheat sheet, heterogeneous achievement group discussion, and homogeneous achievement group discussion with a cheat sheet. One hundred forty-one students enrolled in a required course for teacher education participated in the study and took five regular exams. Students were assigned to groups by the instructor, but were not told the basis of group assignment. The study involved a convenience sample and not one randomly formed. Stratified random sampling formed groups based upon average performance on the first two tests.	The highest scoring grade group was the heterogenous one without a cheat sheet and only discussion involved before students marked their exams independently. Every alternative condition produced higher scores than than when students worked alone. More study was warranted to explain the large gain in scores by low achieving students discussing the test with each other with a cheat (i.e., C's with C's: D's with D's).
Springer, Stanne, and Donovan (2003)	A meta-analysis of 383 studies of college students in science, mathematics, engineering, and technology courses yielded 39 studies included in the meta-analysis. Achievement, persistence, and attitude were the main categories of the studies analyzed with regard to small group learning.	A significant and positive main effect of small group learning on achievement, persistence, and attitude was found. Results support the conclusion that small group learning may greatly influence the academic

Table 1.1 (Continued)

Author(s)	Design	Results\Conclusion
		achievement of under-represented groups and influence greatly the attitude toward learning of women and pre-service teachers in scientific fields.
Sutter and Reid (1969)	In a computer-assisted instruction course, interpersonal and non-interpersonal methods of teaching were investigated for their effect on student attitude and achievement. Pre- and post-test comparisons of attitude and achievement were made for one hundred students randomly assigned to two experimental and one control group.	The experimental groups scored significantly better than the control group. Learning and attitude are affected by interpersonal and non-interpersonal teaching methods.
Taylor and Faust (1952)	One hundred and five students were divided into groups of two and of four and a third group of individuals to determine how efficiency relates to problem solving using groups that differed in size. Over a four day period, both groups worked on four problems and on the fifth day, all groups worked individually on four more problems. The most important score was determined by the number of questions asked by each student in arriving at the correct solution.	The number of questions asked by groups of two and four were not significantly different in reaching a solution to the problems assigned. However, the number of questions asked by individuals was consistently worse than either groups of two or four.

Table 1.1 (Continued)

Author(s)	Design	Results\Conclusion
Tien, Roth, and Kampmeier (2002)	A peer-led team-learning approach was compared to a recitation instructional approach in an organic chemistry class over an eight year period. Variables examined were performance, attitude, and retention.	Statistically significant findings were achieved for all variables. A constructivist based peer-led team is effective in science courses.
Tschumi (1991) (as reported by Felder, 1994)	In an introductory computer science course, students worked alone in one course offering and in two other offerings, different students worked cooperatively. The lecture method was used in the first class and a cooperative method (group work) was used in the other two classes. Would a comparison of performance between the two types of offerings influence achievement and students' attitudes toward group work?	In the fist class, only 36% of the students earned grades of C or higher compared to 58% and 65% of students in the two cooperative classes. The percent of students earning A's in the two cooperative classes was 11.5% versus 6.4% for students who worked alone during the first offering. Students working in groups reportedly had fewer complaints after it was presumably revealed that more students did better working in groups.

Table 1.1 (Continued)

Author (s)	Design	Results\Conclusion
Weinberger, Fischer, and Mandl (2001)	A 2x2 design involving scripted cooperation vs. none scripted cooperation and scaffolding vs. none scaffolding were analyzed relative to individual transfer and equitable knowledge convergence in a text-based computer-mediated communication setting of small groups of three students. Students were assigned three Case problems and had to participate in a mandatory Online learning session that substituted for one class session. Students in the different conditions were all randomly assigned and given three pages of script on theory to be applied to the assigned cases. Students communicated by web-mail discussion boards and worked together within three hours to prepare an evaluation of each case. Students devised their own terms for an analysis of each case. One hundred and five freshmen students in an educational psychology class participated in the semester long study.	Prior training for and changes to a cooperative learning environment can influence equitable convergence of knowledge and individual learning outcomes. Cue-based scripted cooperation and scaffolding in an online learning environment itself promotes learning and discussion more than just open discourse. The interaction of scripted cooperation and scaffolding on knowledge convergence can be fostered by a structured learning discourse. The degree of knowledge convergence may depend on the amount of pre-structuring.
Williams, Carroll, and Hautau (2005)	In each semester for three semesters, different students enrolled in a human development course participated in a study to examine individual accountability within cooperative learning groups. A baseline unit and two	Low and average performing students had similar changes in the way they performed under the three bonus contingencies, but

Table 1.1 (Continued)

Author(s)	Design	Results\Conclusion
	other units were chosen from five content units in the course and used with five to seven member groups that (1) only worked alone during testing, (2) worked in a formal cooperative arrangement on tests, and (3) worked in teams without a formal cooperative structure. During three semesters, students in the cooperative learning arrangement worked under three bonus point arrangements that awarded points based upon how individuals within groups and their groups as a whole performed for a specified amount of improvement. Students were assigned to the five to seven member groups.	high performing students did better under contingencies that (1) awarded partial bonus credit to individuals if the group improved by a certain amount plus full bonus credit to individuals if they improved by a certain amount, and (2) full bonus credit to individuals if both the group and the individual improved their performance by a certain amount.
Zimbardo, Butler, and Wolfe (2003)	In two intro psychology courses taught in consecutive years, students that elected to participate (i.e., 300 in year one and 276 in year two) helped investigators to explore whether team testing would produce superior performance compared to prior alone testing. In the class of 300 students who took the first exam alone, 186 elected to take the second with a partner of choice and 114 took the exam alone. On the third exam, 140 students chose the partner option and 152 took the exam alone. Withdrawals (8) from the course occurred due to factors independent of the study. Of the 276 participants in the	Those taking tests with a partner performed significantly better than those electing to take their exams alone. An average effect size of .80 was achieved in favor of the cooperative team testing format in each of the two classes. Both student elected partners and instructor assigned partners produced positive outcomes in the study.

Table 1.1 (Continued)

Author(s)	Design	Results\Conclusion
	second comparable course, the Partner option was elected by 82 students and 194 students chose the alone option. On the third test, 94 students elected the cooperative team option and 179 students chose to work alone. Three students withdrew from the second course. For both classes, the average of three exam scores determined grades, although a different distribution was computed in order not to penalize those who participated in either option.	

Summary

The several studies presented in Table 1.1 illustrate the depth of interest among researchers interested in cooperative testing and the use or lack of use of structured or unstructured cooperative learning formats as precursors to structured or unstructured cooperative testing events. All of these approaches seem to have one thing in common, however, and that is that achievement gains consistently occur in testing events that feature some degree of cooperation among students. What is next on the horizon is to study in depth the long-term use of a cooperative testing arrangement to determine the conditions within a college environment that may account for the outcomes regularly observed. Obviously, not all of the studies presented here were intended to have this particular goal. Nevertheless, their contribution is that something worth investigating further did happen. Choosing which variables to study and determining and controlling those factors that would make achievement outcomes generalizable across conditions common to college instructional settings is, of course, the most difficult task. In time, more progress will be made toward this end and others who teach at the college level may become convinced enough to try some of these approaches and break ranks with traditional alone testing (Felder and Brent 1994).

2

Cooperative Learning and Testing Principles At Work

In an effort to distinguish between efforts that focus on instruction as a starting point to improve student learning and achievement and efforts that focus on testing formats that also enhance student learning and achievement, certain characteristics of these approaches are described in Figure 2.1. They are presented as opposite ends of the familiar Instruction-Reinforcement-Evaluation Continuum.

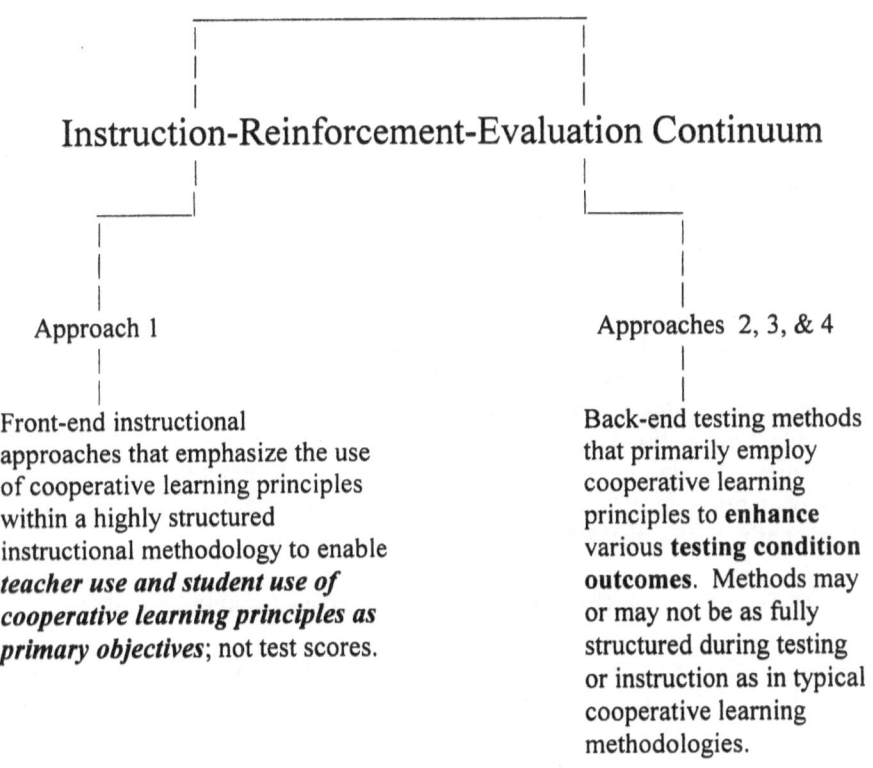

Figure 2.1 Using Different Degrees of Cooperation Within the Instruction-Reinforcement-Evaluation Continuum

(i.e., these elements are common to most teacher's lesson plans).An additional purpose of Figure 2.1 is to emphasize that pathways to learning and achievement vary according to the preferences, practices, and principles of instruction and evaluation favored among those who teach. Hence, few of us will probably ever use the same approaches to instruction just as we currently do not use the same approaches to evaluation. Perhaps this is the way it should be...a constant struggle to achieve the same goal (i.e., student learning and achievement), but somewhat different methods employed in the classroom to achieve these related visions. Figure 2.1 is one representation of how cooperative learning and cooperative testing may be, perhaps, better described as related approaches at work at different ends of the same continuum (Vygotsky 1978; Webb 1997; Zimbardo, Butler, and Wolfe 2003).

Other Features of Approach 1

Groups experience structured cooperative learning methods during instruction. Assigned roles and responsibilities are used and control groups formed by random selection procedures. Groups take individual tests and/or group tests and receive rewards and\or group grades based upon a variety of grading rationales.

Other Features of Alternative Approaches

Approach 2--Little or no cooperative learning used during instruction. Alone and group testing used and students may or may not be encouraged to formally work together to ensure that essential elements of cooperative learning are used within cooperative groups.

Approach 3--Groups work together cooperatively on tests and learn to modify, blend, and adapt the knowledge and experiences they have from existing alone testing orientations in favor of key elements of cooperative learning.

Approach 4--No cooperative learning principles expressly used by the teacher during either instruction or while students are in the testing environment. Students may or may not rely on one another during testing, but may primarily use open books, open notes, legal "cheat" sheets, and take home exam. Other conditions or reward contingencies may also apply.

Different Approaches To Using Cooperative Learning Principles

The variety of studies in Table 1.1 shows differences in degrees to which either none, all, or some of the principles of cooperative learning have been investigated at both the instructional and evaluation ends of teaching. Most studies reviewed here indicated that some type of cooperative arrangement was involved also were studies in which the cooperative arrangement produced not only higher achievement (i.e., 22 studies versus 3), but also produced positive attitudes toward the cooperative condition as a result of experiencing, for example, cooperative group work either before or after traditional testing. Where structured efforts were used in the above studies to help students transition form individual testing strategies and mind sets about which they were already experienced, the studies seem to indicate, from performance outcomes alone, that cooperative learning principles can be taught to students. In turn, these learned principles may often positively influence psychological variables of interest as well (i.e., attitudes, test anxiety, motivation, peer orientation, group interaction and discussions, retention) (Vygotsky 1978; Springer, Stanne, and Donovan 2003; Slavin 1995;1990; Johnson and Johnson 1999 and Jacobs 2000).

Cooperative learning principles used during testing enable students to learn to behave toward each other in productive, task-oriented ways (Slavin 1990; Orbell et al 1988; and Meinster and Rose 1993). In the same manner, students applying cooperative learning principles during testing also become conditioned in ways that enhance their academic and social skills (Johnson, Johnson, and Smith 1991; Smith and Waller 2004). Instructors that choose to focus on the testing environment and facilitate the learning of cooperative learning principles among students may accomplish similar changes in students' test outcomes, social skills building, and attitudes (Meinster and Rose 1993;and Zimbardo et al 2003).

The Cooperative Testing Environment Model

Figure 1.1 is a model showing the cooperative learning principles that have been integrated with teacher-and student-roles to prepare students to work in a cooperative testing environment. When in the testing environment, students put into practice the intra-group habits of mind that are typical of learning to work together in, perhaps, other settings (i.e., in-class sessions and out-of-class sessions where students in cooperative groups pool their abilities to answer review questions typical of those they might encounter on a real test).The instructor facilitates this review process by posing additional questions based upon material covered in class and at moments when students seem not to be cognizant of crucial details needed to enable a correct solution (Vygotsky 1978; Wertsch 1991).This strategy is also akin to one employed by Steinbrink and Jones (1993) in a methodology they describe as cooperative test-review teams. In their method, three to five member teams typically were formed by the teacher, but teams worked together for shorter periods of time (i.e., at least one six-week grading period) than the semester-long cooperative testing groups that produced data for this book. Within the structure of the test-review team method, teams also learned about and practiced the key elements of cooperative learning in ways, the authors felt, teams interacted as described by Johnson and Johnson et al, 1990 (Steinbrink and Jones 1993).Of interest here is that similar trends in higher class mean scores was achieved by students who cooperatively worked in this structured review strategy (Steinbrink and Jones 1993, 1).Positive comments about the usefulness of discussing test review items prior to a test is apparently as valuable to to college-level testing groups as it is to the test review teams studied by others. In

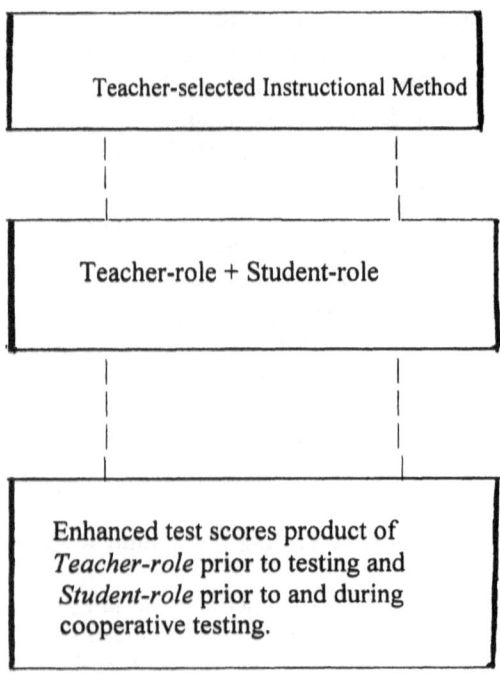

Figure 2.2 The Cooperative Testing Environment Model

In Chapter 4, a review of comments by students who experienced the use of test review items as part of their preparation for group testing may shed further light on factors of this nature in relation to the question of why different cooperative testing arrangements with similar elements tend to produce similar performance and attitudinal outcomes.

Creating a cooperative testing environment has been a growth experience in that, over the years, striving to make cooperative testing accepted among students and peers has led to better ideas that have helped refine what tends to work and not work efficiently for the particular values and beliefs about testing and achievement among professional peers and students at different levels in a college environment. For example, one colleague complained to the department chair that students in her class desired to be tested in groups like those in my class. The assumption here was that cooperative groups were being given an unfair advantage over other students. Moreover, parents of students in other classes apparently were complaining as well. The response offered was to let the other instructor read the literature, as I have done, and then try any methodology with her students. Obviously, a report of findings to interested parents, if desired, might also be a good idea. Result: no takers. On the other end of the spectrum, fortunately, other colleagues have passed by many of my classes during testing and indicated approval of what they witnessed. Encouraged by their comments and, mostly, those of my students, I have continued to use the cooperative testing arrangement even in the face of initial student questions relating to grade determination. Once such student concerns were addressed, reservations abated as the teams looked forward to working in a new testing environment. Again, the focus of the model in Figure 2.2 is to enhance the test performance of cooperative testing groups. The four elements of the model are discussed below.

Teacher-selected Instructional Method

It seems reasonable that lecture discussion, the main technique employed in my classes, would not be an impediment to the use of cooperative learning strategies in college classes where success with such strategies has already been observed (Hanshaw 1982, 15-24). Others (Felder 2001) indicate that a mixture of teaching styles that feature cooperative learning principles that have been blended with, for example, the active learning approach, is a method that works well in his chemical engineering classes. Moreover, other factors involved in the overall instructional process play a role in student learning and performance. For example, Skidmore and Aagaard (1993, 2 of 11)indicate that

> Those challenged with facilitating student learning at all instructional levels recognize that student engagement is key to academic competence. Effecfective study skills are foundationally important to competence in both academic and non-academic settings [sic] (Gettinger & Seibert,2002).These include competencies associated with acquiring, recording, organizing, synthesizing, remembering and using information (Hoover & Patton, 1995).

Pressley & Afflerbach (1995) identified several key strategies that facilitate learning. These included (a) overview before reading,, (b) attention to important information, (c) relating/connecting important points, (d) activation and use of prior knowledge, (e) changing strategies when appropriate, and (f) monitoring understanding and taking action to enhance comprehension. Ideally students who have progressed through formal education systems to the college level have acquired such tactics, strategies and self-regulative skills that direct and enhance their ability to learn. However, students may enter post-secondary level institutions without knowledge of and previous practice with these skills and strategies (Schumacker & Sayler, 1995). Additionally, there seems to be a tradition of bias in the American educational system toward individual accountability and responsibility (Meinster & Rose, 1993). This would seem to inhibit adoption of and engagement in **cooperative** learning endeavors, even though the benefits have been repeatedly demonstrated. However, studies repeatedly show that **cooperative** and collaborative learning environments enhance both classroom climate and student performance (e.g., Aronson, Stephan, Blaney, Sikes, & Snapp, 1978; Webb, 1997).

Johnson and Johnson (1999), however, tend to favor the use of more structured approaches to blending cooperative learning principles with lecturing. This is certainly acceptable. However, when varying periods of time in every class are devoted to questioning and then listening to students' understandings of course material, to using previous exam questions and textbook questions as focal points for discussions during class, and to welcoming students to discuss their own experiences and views in an open discourse in relation to a topic presented, then **lecture-discussion** is being practiced. Students, then, cease being a captive, then, cease being a captive, note taking audience that is un-involved in affecting and constructing their own understandings. Many of the cited problems with the basic lecture, therefore, are avoided with the use of both lecture-discussion and periods of active student involvement as described here. It is also worth noting that the discussion-lecture approach described here also has key elements of the constructivist method of teaching included as described by Brooks and Brooks (1993). For a complete examination of their views, see *In Search of Understanding: The Case For Constructivist Classrooms.* The point here is that among college populations ,there may be a greater expectation that efforts be made on the part of students to help create and to bring their own understandings to the learning table, even though other facilitative efforts are routinely included within a methodology designed to help prepare cooperative teams to perform at a high level during testing.

The Teacher-role in Facilitating the Cooperative Testing Environment

As part of this authors's role in helping to establish among students an understanding of the cooperative testing environment, many actions were consistently taken to facilitate students' adjustment to working together in a testing environment. The following actions constitute the **Teacher-role** shown in Figure 2.2 and are listed below:

(1) *Discuss with students the nature of cooperative learning* as it applies to opportunities to hone their academic and social skills relative to in-class and out-of-class assignments germane to preparing for success on classroom tests. *Review questions* from old exams are useful in helping instructor-formed cooperative teams to self-organize into study groups, to meet at times they decide, and to self-design rules the group agrees to follow along with rules and guidelines the instructor has explained to cooperative groups as a whole. Such review tests also reduce students' anxieties about the variety of questions likely to be encountered (i.e., multiple choice, matching, short to medium open response essay, and completion types) and gave them a focal point for the most relevant types of questions and content that might be encountered (Lambiotte et al, 1987). The number of questions on a typical exam and the changing level of de-tails required to achieve acceptable answers can also be accurately estimated by students using this technique. This instructor facilitated this review process with additional questions in-class and monitored individuals and groups that either seemed to need instructor intervention or that had questions groups did not resolve (i.e., the zone of proximal development at work!). In-class face-to-face interactions of this nature "split the load" between the instructor and individual students and it enabled group members to monitor relative amounts of *individual accountability* with respect to preparatory efforts by group members prior to a test. The same expectations for participation and support have been consistently reported by group members during their self-arranged study sessions. Groups that met tended to share and correct notes freely and at such meetings, some occurring days prior to a test, absent and/or ill group members were able to get caught-up before an upcoming examination. Discussions of test questions outside of class were evident from the questions asked of this instructor once class reconvened. Graduate and undergraduate students who informally came by during office hours provided the anecdotal evidence of the positive nature of meetings outside of class. While this arrangement was not a tightly structured or monitored one, it seemed to work well enough to meet the needs of individuals and to produce positive attitudes and student comments about group testing after testing was completed. Although dissimilar in design when compared to other studies, the overall result of preparing students as described above produced reactions toward group testing as has been found by others (Meinster and Rose 1993; Steinbrink and Jones 1993; Orbell et al 1988).

(2) *Share reprints* and other sources of studies relevant to cooperative test-

ing. In our undergraduate and graduate programs, candidates are routinely required to find and to write summaries of research on various topics. An expansion of these expectations was to invite students to review the research of their professor concerning a methodology used in class that would likely impact their understanding of class content and the grade that might be earned. As a result, copies of research were requested and made available and, at a minimum, positive anticipation prior to group testing turned into positive assessments of how well things worked out immediately after the first group testing experience (i.e., student to student and student to instructor discussions).

(3) Form *teacher-selected, randomly assigned student teams*. After classes began and students were told about the testing arrangement and other information on the syllabus, students were asked to participate in the conditions governing the class. To select groups, a simple random procedure employing the use of an imaginary " X" helped to form all groups. As many as four students per group could be formed from a spot selected before any students came to class. For example, if three to five member groups were best (i.e., actual number decided by class total divided by desired group size), then persons at the ends of the "X" (one to four persons usually selected) formed a group. The person in the center of the "X" would be a member of the next group until all groups desired were formed. In this way strangers and friends were mixed and, presumably, academic abilities and social and emotional variables as well. This process was repeated by choosing another spot. Students closest to the ends of the "X" would form a group if it pointed to vacant seats. Once formed, groups were asked to move nearby to begin exchanging e-mails and phone numbers in order to get acquainted. All groups remained intact for an entire semester for Spring and Fall classes and for five weeks during summer classes. These differences will be taken into consideration when calculating composite mean scores of the alone condition versus the group condition for performance comparisons. No control was instituted for differences in the difficulty of test questions, since the majority of the questions (48/50) in undergraduate classes came from a publisher test bank. For all exams in undergraduate classes, only two or fewer questions were made by this instructor. Even then, the content material and overheads used were always identified prior to a test as material that should be expected on a particular examination. All undergraduate classes met twice a week for 75 minutes. Each half of an exam lasted for approximately 37.5 minutes. Students took two to three exams during the regular sessions with differences due to time constraints for some summer and a few intercession course offerings (i.e., same amount of material covered but fewer exams).Students marked individual exams following discussion of test questions in face-to-face interactions that were encouraged by the instructor prior to each group examination. Alone

testing followed the traditional pattern. Students were also encouraged to not leave the test condition until all it was clear that individual group members no longer needed group support. It was also stressed through out the semester that following the discussion of test questions, whether or not agreement or disagreement occurred, individuals in a group would be held responsible for all answers on a test. Hence, this arrangement provided both individual responsibility, common goal orientation, and group processing of skills in a complex thinking and decision-making environment. This testing environment was in sharp contrast to the "tense, quiet, competitive conditions" typical of most alone examinations discussed in an earlier study (Hanshaw 1982,15-24). Graduate classes took three examinations and the same methodology was used in all classes. All classes were taught by this author. As with undergraduate classes, class size varied from semester to semester. Thirteen undergraduate classes produced an average of 23 students and 18graduate classes averaged 18students over a period from 1998 to 2001. A total of 321students participated in the alone and group testing conditions examined in this book.

(4) *Assist cooperative groups to achieve cohesiveness.* Teachers should discuss the "gold brick"effect as a reasonable example, among others, of why teams may not work as well as planned. Generalize teacher-made rules to include team-made rules established by study groups (i.e., meetings times, class absences, attendance at meetings, and level of participation and preparation acceptable to group members). Reports to the instructor of a team member that is no longer wanted may trigger actions by the instructor to have such a group member take any remaining examinations alone. Groups in this way have some measure of control over how their groups can assist one another to achieve a common goal. In the four year period of data collected for this book, only two persons were reported to the instructor and, after assessing the situation, were told by the instructor that they would have to complete all remaining examinations alone. Such loses did not seem to hinder either performance nor the attitudes of remaining group members. This conclusion seems to be supported by similar findings of others regarding individual concerns within working groups on variables such as preference for cooperative testing (Meinster and Rose 1993) and the (greater) level of concern about group work among high achieving individuals than other achievers (Monk-Turner and Payne 2005).

(5) *Promote cooperative learning and testing blends* or "pure methods" of cooperative learning as part of teaching (Johnson and Johnson 1999; Slavin 1995) and testing for all student populations. Among the majority of students experiencing cooperative learning and testing in my classes, teachers and teacher-to-be were by far the largest populations. These students, par-

ticularly, should be supported and helped to understand that loafers and free-riders in the real-world eventually get their just rewards. Nevertheless, students that help each other and that also help themselves in a collaborative situation should not sacrifice the proven benefits of cooperative testing and/or learning environments because of persons who at times may not live up to the demands of cooperative arrangements. After all, at least from my perspective, many of these participants are or plan to become teachers and may want to try either cooperative learning or cooperative testing methods in their classrooms some day. Personal experience with how to overcome the trials of cooperative efforts is likely to be a valuable asset to those who may teach in either a K-12 or older learning environment.

The Student-role in Promoting Cooperative Testing.

(1) *Students should invest themselves in helping to create a cooperative relationship.* After explaining to students the potential benefits of cooperative learning and cooperative testing, they must be challenged to begin the process of team building by actively participating in completing in-class and out-of-class assignments and be willing to help others benefit from their perspectives on such assignments. Such behaviors build intra-group social skills, provide face-to-face interaction, and revel that group members have placed a premium on working together toward a common goal.

(2) *Students should value the power of open communications.* From a cognitive perspective, students learn that involvement with in-class discussions, out-of-class group work and examination preparation, and many other encounters (e-mail exchanges, phone calls to and from group members, etc.) provides chances for group members to get to know one another, to listen to each others' point of view, and to develop ways to learn to agree and to disagree. They also learn that active involvement in open dialogue, whether in a study group or in a test environment, creates opportunities for them to test their understandings of content material against that of others as they attempt to critically sort out information provided within a group discussion. Within such complex face-to-face exchanges, both graduate and undergraduate students gradually learn to speak-up for what makes sense from their different perspectives. After observing such exchanges for over four years, it is my estimation that the observed frequency of exchanges between group members (i.e., every one pitched in at some point during a semester)and the sheer volume and robustness of observed exchanges across all groups, made it clear that more than one or two individuals were responsible for group outcomes during testing. Such interactive dialogues among college students is consistent with the constructivist's view of learning described as dialectical constructivism (Woolfolk 1998).Hence, helping

students to put a label on their actions, from certain psychological perspectives, helps them to grow in yet other ways that may not have occurred except for their involvement in group experiences encountered during collaborative preparation and during group testing as well. Simply relaying instructor observations to groups at appropriate times is an effective technique that reminds all groups that *they are being monitored.* I have often informed groups of what I have observed about them as I am returning their test papers. Since I have their full attention at that point, this type of feedback works well to reinforce groups that are working well and it encourages groups that are not yet where they want to be.

(3) *Students must be proactive in assessing and reporting their cohesiveness.* Having self-made team rules and enforcing them within groups is a latitude of responsibility given to all cooperative learning and testing groups structured in my classes. Hence, students must utilize their inherent power to manipulate the social and psychological forces operating within a group to maximize group efforts and productive relationships. There are no magic bullets in this regard. From what I have observed over the years, left to their own devices, most cooperative groups have been very effective, in their own way, at getting the most out of group members as I have been using my own rules and techniques of encouragement, feedback, and support of group efforts. Therefore, efforts from both teachers and students, as shown in Figure 2.2, may lead to reaching the common goal of achieving higher test performance and other desired outcomes for both teachers and students.

A Closing Reflection on Approaches to Student Learning and Achievement

Successful paths to student achievement may be limited only by the amount of hard work teachers and students are willing to give to such an outcome. Risk-taking in the form of utilizing testing methodologies that are not traditional is part of the current landscape available to teachers who work in K-12 (see Slavin, 1995 and Johnson and Johnson, 1999) and post-secondary institutions (see reviews of studies in Table 1.1). I have observed over the years that students are more willing to be risk-takers than might be expected. From my experience, if risk-taking (i.e., working in groups) is discussed with students in terms of the relevant research involved, students often become curious and feel that similar outcomes from research involving their class is a similar risk to them. On the other hand, students do show concern about grades and want some control or in-put into how grading will affect participation. That is, students that helped produce the data for this book were given the opportunity to vote on their participation in group testing. I believe the vote was influenced as well by the condition that partners were chosen randomly by the instructor and that students would have the option to record individual answers following group deliberations. Additionally, students must be given an adequate number of opportunities to engage in lengthy testing episodes that will test the fiber of their collective talents. A consistent comment from students is that they felt they were prepared for the tests they took, but indicated that were it not for the group's effort, they would not have done as well if the same group test had been taken alone. Teachers and students, therefore, must act with appropriate attitudes and behaviors that will not diminish contributions to the learning process, regardless of alone or group conditions. However, with regard to group testing, face-to-face interaction and individual responsibility are critical elements to chances for group success.

3

<R̲>
Applying the Cooperative Testing Environment Model In the Classroom

In this chapter, several questions will be addressed regarding the performance of students that worked alone on one half of classroom examinations compared to the performance of the same students that then worked cooperatively on the second half of the same classroom examinations. Each half of all undergraduate examinations lasted 37.5 minutes in a 75 minute class period and 75 minutes each half in graduate classes. All examinations were administered by this author (i.e., three examinations in every class, except in EDCI 601, 2001, with 18 students that took only two examinations). Undergraduate classes met twice a week and all graduate classes met once a week. As mentioned earlier, all cooperative groups were randomly formed and stayed together for an entire semester.

Three key questions guided the analysis of data collected from eighteen classes. The key questions were: (1) How do the mean composite scores of students working alone compare to the mean composite scores of the same students working in cooperative groups?; (2) What is the magnitude of the effect size for students working in the cooperative condition?; and (3) Is there information in the data that might indicate what is occurring within cooperative testing groups within a particular class so that further understandings might be gained regarding how these subgroups performed or interacted beyond what a comparison of means might tell? In the sections to follow, relevant portions of analyses performed on the data collected for all classes will be used to address each of the above questions.

Question 1: What are the mean composite score comparisons between the Alone and Cooperative testing conditions?

Table 3.1 presents the results of a One-Way Analysis of Variance of the alone and cooperative group scores from 321 students enrolled in both graduate and undergraduate courses. One hundred forty students were undergraduates (i.e., in seven classes) and one hundred eighty-one students were earning graduate degrees (i.e., in 11 classes). The courses were taken by these students between 1999 and 2001. Data for each class was analyzed separately and descriptive statistics for each class are presented along with F-ratio and probability results for the comparison of means

Table 3.1 Analysis of Composite Alone and Cooperative Group Test Scores

Class (yr)	Alone Mean SD (N=)	Group Mean SD (N=)	Multivariate Test Results F-ratio	p =	Shared Variance or Eta² (η^2)	Cooperative Condition Effect Size ($1-\eta^2$)
EDPY 303 (1999)	222.5455 21.8088 (11)	218.5455 23.6532 (11)	.125	.731	.012	.988
EDPY 303 (1999)	224.3571 27.7117 (14)	265.5000 12.8047 (14)	22.920	.000 *	.638	.362
EDCI 601 (1999)	266.1667 13.3405 (12)	283.9167 6.6258 (12)	28.441	.000 *	.721	.279
EDCI 601 (1999)	253.5405 20.9756 (37)	272.5405 20.0147 (37)	24.503	.000 *	.405	.595
EDPY 303 (2000)	243.5385 19.4674 (26)	273.4231 7.5322 (26)	47.193	.000 *	.654	.346
EDCI 601 (2000)	272.8000 14.8084 (10)	288.4000 4.0332 (10)	10.185	.011 *	.531	.469

Table 3.1 Analysis of Composite Alone and Cooperative Group Test Scores (Continued)

Class (yr)	Alone Mean SD (N=)	Group Mean SD (N=)	Multivariate Test Results F-ratio	p =	Shared Variance or Eta² (η^2)	Cooperative Condition Effect Size ($1-\eta^2$)
EDCI 601 (2000)	263.000 12.8755 (10)	277.4000 7.0427 (10)	29.051	.000 *	.763	.237
EDCI 601 (2001)	263.000 17.6068 (13)	275.8462 25.1855 (13)	6.531	.025 *	.352	.648
EDCI 601 (2001)	256.5333 25.8038 (15)	275.4000 6.4896 (15)	7.927	.014 *	.362	.638
EDCI 601 (2001)	277.9412 13.8043 (17)	286.6471 12.0827 (17)	17.537	.001 *	.523	.477
EDCI 601 (2001)	193.1667 5.5227 (18)	197.5000 2.4555 (18)	7.601	.013 *	.309	.691
EDCI 601 (2001)	274.4762 12.7107 (21)	293.5238 2.9431 (21)	49.717	.000 *	.713	.287

Table 3.1 Analysis of Composite Alone and Cooperative Group Test Scores (Continued)

Class (yr)	Alone Mean SD (N=)	Group Mean SD (N=)	Multivariate Test Results F-ratio	p =	Shared Variance or Eta² (η^2)	Cooperative Condition Effect Size ($1-\eta^2$)
EDPY 303 (2001)	248.4706 17.7310 (17)	271.5294 9.6638 (17)	36.885	.000 *	.697	.303
EDPY 303 (2001)	135.2083 33.0599 (24)	180.0000 14.1175 (24)	59.185	.000 *	.720	.280
EDPY 303 (2001)	252.5806 22.3201 (31)	271.9355 14.8188 (31)	19.569	.000 *	.395	.605
EDPY 307 (2001)	204.8235 24.7594 (17)	245.4706 15.2607 (17)	36.896	.000 *	.698	.302
EDRS 605 (2001)	244.3846 37.2504 (13)	288.3077 10.2257 (13)	21.438	.001 *	.641	.359
EDRS 605 (2001)	264.6000 18.2632 (15)	291.8667 5.4493 (15)	35.703	.000 *	.718	.282

for each class. Additionally, shared variance results (i.e., Eta² values) and effect size results (Wilks' Lambda in relation to Eta² ([i.e., η^2]) are also shown (i.e., Wilks' Lambda (λ) = 1-η^2). These correlations helped to determine the influence of alone condition scores on cooperative condition scores (i.e., shared variance) as well as the influence of the cooperative condition by itself (i.e., 1-η^2) values. The probability level used for significance was p =.05 using SPSS for Windows: Analyzing and Understanding Data, 2nd ed., by Green, Salkind, and Akey (Upper Saddle River, NJ: Prentice Hall, 2000). The design employed with the Cooperative Testing Environment Model was the Treatment-by-Subjects or Repeated Measures Design (Bruning and Kintz 1969, 43)."The reason for using the treatment-by subjects design is usually simply to increase the precision of the experiment by eliminating inter-subject differences as a source of error"(Lindquist 1953, 156).Please note that an *asterisk (*)* in Table 3.1 indicates that the *composite cooperative condition mean was significantly greater* than the composite alone condition mean.

Conclusions

Clearly the results shown in Table 3.1 overwhelmingly support the conclusions of previous research (Hanshaw 1982) that indicated the superiority of cooperative testing over individualistic testing. Although previous research (i.e.,Table 1.1)differed from this research with regard to variables examined and methodologies used, it is still evident that achievement for students working in groups was consistently higher, regardless of overall class size. Students in seventeen of the eighteen classes in this research earned not only higher composite mean scores in the cooperative condition, but they also earned cooperative group scores that were significantly different from those earned in the alone or individualistic condition by a 17:1 ratio. The cooperative group condition means were significant at or beyond the .01 level in sixteen of the eighteen classes examined.

Based upon observations of and the judgments made about the ways in which cooperative testing groups interacted, many helpful insights have been gained. Among the many beliefs formed from working with cooperative testing groups is that a consistent belief in the cooperative testing condition *among students* is highly dependent upon (1) allowing students to record separate answers following face-to-face interactions during testing, and (2) allowing students to have rules of their design that help students to manage their "collective investment" in the success of the random groups to which they get assigned for an entire semester. This level of accountability for individual decision-making and student input into rules used to judge the behavior expected within instructor-formed groups appears to balance over time to make groups work well enough to support high academic achievement for both group members and individuals; higher achievement, even, than what most students said they probably would have achieved alone.

Having drawn the above conclusions based upon both observations and beliefs drawn from experiences working with college-level cooperative groups for several years is perhaps not enough evidence for skeptics of cooperative testing. Additional evidence, however, will be presented in the form of data related to "intra-group position changes". This data strongly supports the idea that within cooperative groups there exists a mixture of up and down, and sometimes constant, performance among members of such groups. These *collective changes* among interdependent group members appears to be related to the strength of the cooperative condition during testing. Again, this inferential assessment will be further examined by the data presented in response to related questions two and three that are addressed in the next sections of this book.

Question 2: What are the effect size estimates for the Alone and Cooperative testing conditions?

As shown in Table 3.1, the shared variance between the alone and cooperative conditions is expressed in terms of the correlational statistic Eta². "Eta² is related to Wilks' Lambda", also a correlational statistic, "by the equation $1-\eta^2 = \lambda$" (Green, Salkind, and Akey 2000, 208-211). Eta² is also symbolized as η^2. "η^2 can be interpreted just like r^2. It is the proportion of variance in the dependent variable that is related to the independent variable" (Thorndike and Dinnel 2001, 433-436). The composite alone score in this data is the independent variable and the composite cooperative group score is the dependent variable. Readers are reminded that when the F-ratio shows a significant result for the comparison of means, the associated Wilks' Lamda and the multivariate Eta² values produced are also statistically significant (Green, Salkind, and Akey 2000, 208-217).

Conclusions

The average Effect Size across all 18 classes where students worked in the cooperative condition was $\lambda=.453$. As a correlational statistic that can be interpreted as an r^2 value, the value $\lambda=.453$ indicates that the cooperative testing condition had an effect size that can be described as large (.67). For example, the square root of .453 yields an **r**-value used here to give *descriptive interpretation* to the Wilks' Lambda effect sizes shown in Table 3.1 (see also, Cohen 1988, 75-83). The descriptive interpretations of small, medium, and large are used here to give a convenient interpretation to the correlational nature of the two statistics reported for this data. The medium to large effect sizes for the cooperative condition across eighteen classes indicates the powerful effect of the cooperative condition with the influence of the alone condition removed. It is also worth noting that in the one class (i.e., see Table 3.1) where there was no significant difference between the means, the cooperative condition still produced a large effect size (r=.99).

Another interesting view of this same data is the picture presented by looking at the median as way to describe the effect sizes produced by the cooperative testing condition in each of the 18 classes examined. Thus, from the data in Table 3.1, it can be seen that the cooperative testing condition produced significant effect sizes that ranged from .237 to .988. The **median** value for the effect size of the cooperative testing condition was calculated to be .361. This means that nine of the 18 classes were below the median of .361 and nine were above .361. Hence, the nine lowest effect sizes can be described as "medium to large" and as "large" for the nine highest effect sizes. Apparently the cooperative testing condition is a viable method of improving student performance whether in graduate or undergraduate classes or as disciplines or content vary.

Question 3: What are the insights that might be gained from an examination of sub-groups within a class that worked in the cooperative testing condition?

The analysis of data for students that worked in the alone and cooperative testing conditions is shown in Table 3.2. The strategy devised to determine what, if anything, was occurring within the various sub-groups within a class involved (a) determining whether each student's performance either stayed the same, went up, or went down following the administration of all exams by the end of the semester for a given class. These performance variations are designated 1st, 2nd, 3rd, etc., for each student's alone and cooperative condition score results following that student's number designation. For example, if a student appeared on my roll as the first student in a sub-group, then that student would be S1 and the numbers following that designation describe that student's position after all alone and cooperative testing were completed. In this way, performance changes from the alone and cooperative conditions (i.e., composite scores) could be used to track intra-group position changes for each student. This was an important outcome to investigate because in previous research (Zimbardo et al, 2003; Webb, 1987; and Meinster and Rose, 1993, among others) all of these authors raised concerns relative to who benefits most from cooperative testing or whether the benefits are equally spread out. Although the analysis done here may not address all of these concerns, it may enhance the knowledge base regarding how individual students perform in groups when they are free to record their own answers as a result of group face-to-face interactions within the context of a common goal orientation. The stipulation of *not requiring common answers* by cooperative group members may be one reason why, at least in this research, different benefits accrue to students within the same cooperative groups; even though they all had access to the same pool of interactively contributed group information during cooperative testing. The assumption here, of course, is that individual group members consistently were prepared for each test taken and that individuals within a group made consistent efforts to make certain every group member understood the answers provided within a cooperative group. Time taken by a group to discuss answers offered by group members and other factors associated with a testing episode (i.e., environmental as well as learning style preferences) were variables in this model that were not controlled for any sub-group. Hence, one might surmise that individual performance, in large measure, might depend upon how well an individual's decision-making functioned under the influence of a particular cooperative testing arrange-

Table 3.2 Intra-Group Position Changes

Class (yr) (N=)	Composite Alone Testing Position	Composite Group Testing Position	Results of Intra-Group Position Change
EDPY303 (1999) (14)	S1-2nd S2-1st S3-3rd	S1-2nd S2-3rd S3-1st	Intra-group position improved for (1/3) (*one-out-of* three students). Two students had higher group composite scores compared to composite alone scores.
	S1-1st S2-2nd	S1-2nd S2-1st	Intra-group position improved for (½) students. Both students had higher composite group scores than composite alone scores.
	S1-3rd S2-2nd S3-1st	S1-1st S2-1st S3-1st	Intra-group position improved for (2/3) students. All students ended with composite group scores > than composite alone scores.
	S1-1st S2-3rd S3-2nd	S1-1st S2-2nd S3-2nd	Intra-group positions improved for (1/3) students. all students had composite group scores > than composite alone scores.
	S1-2nd S2-3rd S3-1st	S1-2nd S2-1st S3-3rd	Intra-group position improved for (1/3) students. All students had composite group scores > than composite alone scores.
EDPY 303 (1999) (11)	S1-4th S2-2nd S3-3rd S4-1st	S1-1st S2-3rd S3-2nd S4-2nd	Intra-group position improved for (1/4) students. All students had composite group scores > than composite alone scores.
	S1-3rd S2-1st S3-4th S4-2nd	S1-1st S2-2nd S3-4th S4-3rd	Intra-group position improved for (1/4) students. *None* of the students had composite group scores >

Table 3.2 Intra-Group Position Changes (Continued)

Class (yr) (N=)	Composite Alone Testing Position	Composite Group Testing Position	Results of Intra-Group Position Change
	S1-2nd S2-3rd S3-1st	S1-1st S2-2nd S3-3rd	than composite alone scores. Intra-group position improved for (2/3) students. Only one student ended with a composite group score greater than the composite alone score.
EDCI 601 (1999) (37)	S1-1st S2-3rd S3-2nd	S1-1st S2-3rd S3-1st	Intra-group position improved for (1/3) students All students ended with a composite group score greater than the composite alone score.
	S1-3rd S2-1st S3-2nd	S1-3rd S2-1st S3-2nd	No students changed their Intra-group position (0/3). All students ended with composite group scores > than composite alone scores.
	S1-2nd S2-1st	S1-1st S2-1st	Intra-group position improved for (½) students. Both students had greater composite group scores compared to composite alone scores.
	S1-2nd S2-1st S3-3rd	S1-1st S2-2nd S3-2nd	Intra-group position improved for (2/3) students. All students ended with composite group scores > than composite alone scores.
	S1-2nd S2-3rd S3-1st S4-3rd	S1-4th S2-1st S3-3rd S4-1st	Intra-group position improved for (2/4) students. All students ended with composite group scores > than composite alone scores.
	S1-1st S2-2nd	S1-1st S2-1st	Intra-group position improved for (½) students.

Table 3.2 Intra-Group Position Changes (Continued)

Class (yr) (N=)	Composite Alone Testing Position	Composite Group Testing Position	Results of Intra-Group Position Change
	S1-1st S2-3rd S3-2nd	S1-1st S2-2nd S3-3rd	Both students ended with composite group scores > than composite alone scores. Intra-group position improved for (1/3) students. All students ended with composite group scores > than composite alone scores.
	S1-3rd S2-2nd S3-1st	S1-3rd S2-2nd S3-1st	Intra-group position did not improve for any students (0/3). Only one student ended with a composite group score < than the composite alone score.
	S1-3rd S2-1st S3-2nd S4-4th	S1-2nd S2-4th S3-1st S4-3rd	Intra-group position improved for (3/4) students. Only one student ended with a composite group score > the composite alone score.
	S1-2nd S2-1st S3-2nd S4-4th	S1-1st S2-2nd S3-2nd S4-1st	Intra-group position improved for (2/4) students. All students ended with composite group scores > than composite alone scores.
	S1-1st S2-3rd S3-2nd	S1-3rd S2-2nd S3-1st	Intra-group position improved for (1/3) students. Only one student had a composite group score > than the composite alone score.
	S1-2nd S2-3rd S3-1st	S1-3rd S2-2nd S3-1st	Intra-group position improved for (1/3) students. All students ended with composite group scores > than composite alone scores.
EDCI 601 (1999)	S1-4th S2-3rd	S1-1st S2-1st	Intra-group position improved for (3/4) students.

Table 3.2 Intra-Group Position Changes (Continued)

Class (yr) (N=)	Composite Alone Testing Position	Composite Group Testing Position	Results of Intra-Group Position Change
(12)	S3-1st S4-2nd	S3-1st S4-1st	All cooperative condition composite scores > than composite alone scores.
	S1-1st S2-2nd S3-3rd S4-4th	S1-1st S1-2nd S3-1st S4-4th	Intra-group position improved for (1/4) students. All cooperative condition composite scores > than alone composite scores.
	S1-3rd S2-2nd S3-4th S4-1st	S1-2nd S2-3rd S3-3rd S4-1st	Intra-group position improved for (2/4) students. All cooperative condition composite scores > than alone composite scores.
EDPY 303 (2000) (26)	S1-2nd S2-3rd S3-1st	S1-1st S2-1st S3-2nd	Intra-group position improved for (2/3) students. All cooperative condition composite scores > than alone condition composite scores.
	S1-1st S2-2nd	S1-1st S2-2nd	Intra-group position did improve for either student (0/2). All composite group scores > than composite alone scores.
	S1-1st S2-2nd	S1-1st S2-2nd	Intra-group position did not improve for either student (0/2). All composite group scores > than composite alone scores.
	S1-1st S2-3rd S3-2nd S4-1st	S1-2nd S2-1st S3-3rd S4-1st	Intra-group position improved for (1/4) students. All composite group scores greater than composite alone scores.
	S1-2nd	S1-1st	Intra-group position

Table 3.2 Intra-Group Position Changes (Continued)

Class (yr) (N=)	Composite Alone Testing Position	Composite Group Testing Position	Results of Intra-Group Position Change
	S2-3rd S3-1st S4-4th	S2-3rd S3-1st S4-2nd	improved for (2/4) students. All composite group scores > than composite alone scores.
	S1-3rd S2-2nd S3-5th S4-4th S5-1st	S1-1st S2-2nd S3-5th S4-3rd S5-4th	Intra-group position improved for (2/4) students. All composite group scores were greater than composite alone scores.
	S1-3rd S2-1st S3-4th S4-2nd	S1-2nd S2-3rd S3-1st S4-3rd	Intra-group position improved for (2/4) students. All cooperative condition composite scores were > than composite alone condition scores.
	S1-1st S2-1st	S1-2nd S2-1st	Intra-group position did not improve for either student (0/2). All composite group scores were > than composite alone scores.
EDCI 601 (2000) (10)	S1-3rd S2-1st S3-2nd	S1-1st S2-1st S3-2nd	Intra-group position improved for (1/3) students. All composite group scores were > than composite alone scores.
	S1-1st S2-1st S3-2nd	S1-1st S2-1st S3-1st	Intra-group position improved for (1/3) students. All composite group scores were > than composite alone scores.
	S1-1st S2-3rd S3-2nd S4-2nd	S1-1st S2-1st S3-1st S4-2nd	Intra-group position improved for (2/4) students. All composite group scores were > than composite alone scores.

Table 3.2 Intra-Group Position Changes (Continued)

Class (yr) (N=)	Composite Alone Testing Position	Composite Group Testing Position	Results of Intra-Group Position Change
EDCI 601 (2001) (17)	S1-1st S2-2nd S3-4th S4-3rd	S1-1st S2-2nd S3-3rd S4-4th	Intra-group position improved for (**1/4**) students. All composite group scores were > than composite alone scores.
	S1-1st S2-4th S3-2nd S4-3rd	S1-1st S2-2nd S3-1st S4-1st	Intra-group position improved for (**3/4**) students. All composite group scores were > than composite alone scores.
	S1-1st S2-2nd S3-3rd	S1-2nd S2-3rd S3-1st	Intra-group position improved for (**1/3**) students. All composite group scores were > than composite alone scores.
	S1-1st S2-3rd S3-2nd	S1-1st S2-1st S3-2nd	Intra-group position improved for (**1/3**) students. Only two students had ended with composite group scores greater than composite alone scores.
	S1-2nd S2-3rd S3-1st	S1-2nd S2-1st S3-2nd	Intra-group position improved for (**1/3**) students. All composite group scores were > than composite alone scores.
EDPY 303 (2001) (17)	S1-1st S2-2nd	S1-1st S2-2nd	Intra-group position did not change for either student (**0/2**). Both students ended with composite group scores > than composite alone scores.
	S1-4th S2-2nd S3-1st S4-2nd	S1-4th S2-2nd S3-3rd S4-1st	Intra-group position improved for (**1/4**) students. All composite group scores were > than composite

Table 3.2 Intra-Group Position Changes (Continued)

Class (yr) (N=)	Composite Alone Testing Position	Composite Group Testing Position	Results of Intra-Group Position Change
	S1-3rd S2-5th S3-1st S4-4th S5-2nd	S1-1st S2-3rd S3-4th S4-5th S5-2nd	alone scores. Intra-group position improved for (2/5) students. All composite group scores >composite alone scores. Intra-group position improved for (2/5) students. All composite group scores were > than composite alone scores.
	S1-4th S2-2nd S3-1st S4-3rd	S1-1st S2-1st S3-2nd S4-1st	Intra-group position improved for (3/4) students. All composite group scores were > than composite alone scores.
	S1-2nd S2-1st	S1-2nd S2-1st	Intra-group position did not improve for either student (0/2). Both students ended with composite group scores > than composite alone scores.

ment. Table 3.2 may provide insights into just this question.

Discussion of Intra-Group Improved Position Change Data

The results of changes in composite test scores that occurred between testing conditions is shown Table 3.2. It must be made clear that this analysis is based upon only *eight* of the eighteen classes or 144 (44.9%) of the 321 students studied. This severely limits any conclusions that may be drawn from the behavior of students working in sub-groups within a class. Fortunately, only group assignment data was lost and not records of test grades or there would not have been any way to assign final grades to students in eight classes!! What a headache that would have caused. Nevertheless, this analysis of the partial data recovered (i.e., there was an apparent price paid for two office moves) paints an interesting portrait of the up and down nature of student achievement within alone and cooperative groups.

Analysis of Intra-Group Improved Position Change Data

The objective of the analysis of data shown in Table 3.2 was to produce a regression equation from which one could predict, for any given cooperative subgroup size, the average number of students within a sub-group that might likely *upwardly* improve in performance. To achieve this objective, all of the decimal equivalents of the fractions shown in bold print and the sizes of the sub-groups that produced these numbers were tabulated to produce a scatter plot (see Salkind's *Statistics For People Who (Think They) Hate Statistics*, 2000, pp. 109-122). While the scatter plot was informative, the regression equation produced by the procedure Salkind indicated was the principal product desired. The particular regression equation produced from the forty-four sub-groups within eight classes was

$$Y = .114 (X) + .002278.$$

The regression of group size as the independent variable and improved position change as the dependent variable was $F(1,42) = 8.846$, $p = .005$ and $t(42) = 2.974$, $p = .005$; a significant result. Additionally, as expected, the correlation between sub-group size and improved position change was positive (.417) with a degree of error (i.e., for subgroup sizes not close to the regression line) equal to .2060. The above equation indicates, for example, that for a mythical group of three students, the predicted number of students in such a group that might upwardly change in performance would be as follows:

$$Y = .114 (3) + .002278$$
$$Y = .344 \text{ (i.e., the logical meaning is one person).}$$

Now, compare the predicted value of .344 to the actual value of .37 calculated by adding up the improved position change data for the 18 sub-groups that had only groups of three students and dividing that total by 18. Nice tool, yes?

The prediction of performance from an equation like the one above, also might indicate that further refinements to a particular testing arrangement should be considered..In other words, the fractions in bold print indicate the number of sub-group members that actually increased their level of performance relative to other students in the same sub-group. These fractions are not a measure, for example, of students who maintained the same relative position compared to other students in the same sub-group whether or not they had the top score. The fraction only measures the number of students who moved from, say, 4th place to 2nd place and not those that started in 1st place or 2nd place and ended there when composite alone test scores were compared to composite cooperative group scores at the end of all testing for a particular sub-group. Ideally, then, knowing how sub-groups have performed in the past could lead to considerations by an instructor that might change or improve the number of average and low performing students within cooperative groups the next time cooperative testing is instituted in a class. Such information also could help to close the loop in the familiar instruction-reinforcement-evaluation paradigm mentioned earlier, since *feedback* from test performance is an established way that teachers better inform the instruction given to their students. But what about the students that maintained a high level of performance in both the alone and cooperative conditions relative to others in the same group? That is, what about a student who was the top performer in both the alone and cooperative testing conditions? Using this methodology, such performance would not be counted as an "improved position change". Even so, such performance carries additional rewards in ways other than being distinctively higher than other composite scores. The "other" benefits to top performing students is that they would likely enjoy knowing that their face-to-face interactions and support of a common goal orientation played a meaningful role in helping others and themselves to achieve within a cooperative group setting *without*, apparently, sacrificing their own high achievement. Such an outcome, though conditioned, perhaps, on other factors, is *exactly* the disposition toward teaching and helping others that is desired within our school of education and, no doubt, within others as well. If practicing and teachers-to-be learn such behaviors as a part of cooperative learning and testing environments, then such instructional and testing methodologies self-define their value and applicability when instituted in classrooms.

Slavin (1995, 67) makes a more global point in his discussion of the benefits-reward"concepts discussed above. Specifically, he indicates that when indices of the cooperative condition such as altruism, equality, and competition are examined for those students who have worked in a cooperative setting, researchers (i.e.,Hertz-Lazarowitz, Sharan, and Steinberg, 1980) showed that "students who had experienced Group Investigation made more altruistic choices than did control students" and that when students were "reassigned to new groups for an experimental task, they cooperated better and their groups had higher productivity than groups made up from the control classes". Although a replication study (Sharan et al., 1984) did not confirm the findings of the prior 1980 study, Slavin points out that Sharan et al did find that "when new groups were made up from students in the experimental and control classes, there was more verbal and nonverbal cooperation and less competition on a construction task among students who had experienced Group Investigation than among control students". The parallels of benefits and rewards among the different populations of interest to various researchers are important in their implications for both K-12 populations and students in higher education; some of them, in the latter category, teachers in our schools. Obviously, much more is at stake for students in cooperative testing arrangements than just making the highest score. As the above research indicates, there is an equally important human development component involved as well. Perhaps comments from students in Chapter 4 will further underscore the rewards and benefits of cooperative testing that are also a part of the overall achievement/learning landscape.

Applications of Cooperative Testing in Science Classes

As a chemistry science educator, it is important to remind teachers of science of the applicability of cooperative group testing to science classes. This will be done by reiterating the results of earlier work that has already appeared in the literature (Hanshaw 1982, 15-24)and summarized in this work as well (i.e., in case you missed it, see pages 14 and 15).There are, however, some details that were not critical to thereview that may be critical to readers that desire to try cooperative testing. For example, in the original study, separate classrooms for alone and cooperative testing were used but in today's high schools and in many college classrooms this may not be an option because of space limitations. In the present study, students took their first half of an examination alone and the cooperative testing half last in the same room. This seemed to be a good a good arrangement so that alone testing would follow the traditional pattern just like testing in classes where no cooperative examinations occurred. What ever you decide to do, I hope that you will try cooperative testing. If your experience turns out to be anything near to what has happened in my classes, it is likely that you will prefer cooperative testing as well. Have other teachers of science used this methodology and, if so, what did they find? Well, I'm glad you asked !! In the section that follows, a summary of a specialist degree field study performed by one of my former graduate students answers these questions and should be evidence of what is possible, hopefully, even in the more tightly controlled environment of high schools; college instructors usually don't have control as an issue. Since testing in this manner will probably draw some attention to how you evaluate students in your classroom, be prepared to inform inquiring minds as to the soundness of cooperative learning and testing by either using the information in this book or other sources of your choosing. If there are any questions and/or comments about trying cooperative testing, at either educational level, you may reach me at lhanshaw@ olemiss.edu. Good Luck!.

A Science Teacher's Specialist Field Study

Applying cooperative testing and cooperative learning to K-12 environments furthers research at this level. Of interest here is a study that involved high school Biology I students working in a cooperative testing environment. According to Hodges (1976), the teacher of the class, students in the randomly assigned control group class (i.e., seven females and sixteen males) and students in the experimental group class (i.e., seventeen females and seven males) were given identical teacher-made tests during a typical six-weeks period. The school's guidance counselor gave students an attitude inventory used in the study. Initial randomization was the result of the way students were assigned to their classes by the school's computer. A second random assignment was done by the teacher to assign classes of students to either the experimental group or the control group by drawing numbers from a container that would represent the two classes used in the study from the four classes in biology at the school. Hodges concluded in her study that "students who worked in the cooperative condition scored significantly higher on test performance than those students who did not experience the cooperative condition. The study supports the use of cooperative learning as an alternative in the classroom. Although the attitude analysis showed no significant difference, the experimental students did move from not liking biology to a neutral state which indicated improvement on the evaluation sub-scale"(1996, 24). It is commendable that a high school administration and a teacher were able to collaborate in the interest of research of this type. I hope that this important recognition of the importance of research by school practitioners continues. Other teachers, whether or not they teach science, are invited to engage in their own experiments to explore both the likely rewards of cooperative testing as well as any psychological variables of interest to them.

4

Cooperative Classroom Testing: Qualitative Considerations

The comments of students who experienced cooperative testing is an important source of insights for describing how students view perceived benefits of participating in cooperative testing. For example, much of the discussion of the various components of cooperative testing presented in Figure 1.1 was based upon undergraduate reactions to the cooperative testing arrangement described in this book. Notes and recollections of conversations with students enabled me to convey what has already been presented. While these views furthered my understanding and appreciation of cooperative testing and learning, there were, of course, graduate students and practicing teachers who directly expressed similar views. More of what all students had to say would have been possible had there not been a transition toward the use of electronic data gathering of course evaluations. This, at times, complicated and severely limited direct access to original student comments. Nevertheless, I hope that I have given a fair representation to the many informative and encouraging comments from undergraduates and graduate students alike.

In the years following 2001, however, students in all of my classes have taken only group tests. Because of this change in methodology, no test scores of students after 2001 were included in the data presented in Chapter Three. These data will be presented in a separate publication.

Nevertheless, the comments and reactions of current students regarding cooperative testing mirror similar comments of students from earlier years. Because nearly all students have already experienced a long history of taking examinations alone, presenting the comments of students who only took group tests is not, therefore, viewed as a confounding factor. Hence, I have taken some license in presenting these qualitative views, since the absence of alone testing, about which students are already familiar, probably does not meaningfully change students' feelings about cooperative testing.

Additionally, but for very different reasons, I hope readers will appreciate the gravity of the views of practicing K-12 educators and graduate students, since this group is also the most likely ones to immediately utilize some form of cooperative testing in their own classrooms. Moreover, the opinions and perceptions of persons who already have classroom teaching responsibilities and who have experienced cooperative testing need to be heard. Such viewpoints may be encouraging to both K-12 teachers and college faculty who have not yet tried cooperative testing and learning arrangements. With only minor editing, Table 4.1 presents comments taken

Table 4.1 Portfolio Comments of Teachers and Graduate Students

Student	Comment
S1	A unique approach to test taking was used in this course. We were divided into small groups and a collaborative test taking approach was used. Group testing actually caused me to study even harder than normal so that I would excel in the group. No one wanted to let their group down by not being prepared and we all worked hard to understand the material. This caused us to work cooperatively and to get to know the other people in our group. If we disagreed on an answer, the group discussed the possibilities and arrived at a mutual conclusion. The group testing definitely brought out the best in me. As a result of being in a group, I studied extremely hard, typed all of my notes after each class, and made study guides. I obtained an A in this class and felt I deserved the grade.
S2	[Larry, I thought you would enjoy this. It came from a master's candidate's portfolio I was grading. *Kerry* (i.e.,a School of Education colleague)]. This has been the only class where I've been able to take a group test. This enabled interaction between all group members. Everyone had a part to play. In the event that one forgot something, there was another to pick up the slack. We communicated inside as well as outside of the classroom concerning numerous issues. As a group, we had to decide what was best for the group as a whole. After the group testing, I thought it to be such a good idea that I tried it with my students. They loved it. It gave everyone the chance to feel bright. My students learned how to work together and how to help one another.
S3	During this course we had two tests and a final research paper. The tests were not like any others I have had in education or as a student in other classes. They were taken as a group. This proved what some research has said about cooperative testing in that more material can be retained through working together and being test-ed as a group. It made it hard to study, since I did not know what types of questions would be on the test. But all in all, working to-gether not only made me study harder for the others

Table 4.1 Portfolio Comments of Teachers and Graduate Students (Continued)

Student	Comment
	in my group, it also comforted me because I had a few others to fall back on to discuss things with if my mind froze up.
S4	Our examinations were given to us as groups. Taking a test with my peers gave me confidence because each member brought his or her own strengths to the group. The content tested was very complex and I found it very easy to become overwhelmed. Another course requirement was to write a paper on one of the major concepts covered in our text. I chose to do mine on leadership, since I plan to become a principal in the near future. I really enjoyed this assignment and class as a whole. The exams in this course were the most difficult and challenging evaluations that I have ever encountered. However, I learned a lot of valuable information and an A in the course.
S5	I like the testing technique because the teacher incorporated team testing during the testing period..
S6	We had a lot of practice with our communication skills because we were allowed to take group testing. We all studied the informa-tion individually, but collaborated to create the best possible answer to each question on the test. It was a wonderful experience. I've never had the privilege to group test, so this was indeed a novel experience. Open discussion questions always led to heated debates because of different views and opinions. These discussions help in real life situations. The experiences of others help us to deal with our own situations. Overall, we learned a lot from each other just by communicating constantly during class.
S7	After the first test, let students vote on whether they want group or individual tests.
S8	Several assessments were given using the cooperative learning approach. We were evaluated in a group setting in which we had to communicate in order to do well on our assessment. The teacher asked test questions that forced students to use their

56   Qualitative Considerations About Cooperative Testing

Table 4.1 Portfolio Comments of Teachers and Graduate Students (Continued)

Student	Comment
	critical thinking skills. As a result of taking this course, I will give a lot more thought to the curriculum. I will have students work in groups while I walk around and monitor them. I also will give students projects to determine their learning styles.
S9	Communication and cooperation were addressed in two ways for this course. I completed tests within designated groups. We discussed questions with one another until we arrived at the best answer. I actually learned a lot as I took the test. The other way I communicated and cooperated in this course was through class lecture and discussion.
S10	I truly learned from and enjoyed the interactive group learning and problem solving method. This was my first experience with testing of this nature. It provided positive feed-back and encouragement as a form of evaluation.
S11	The two classes that I took under Dr. Hanshaw definitely stressed communication and cooperation. I was given the opportunity to take cooperative tests in his classes. I needed the ability to communicate my ideas and to cooperate with my group members in order to succeed in the classes. These classes showed me that new techniques such as cooperative testing can also be used in the elementary classroom.
S12	Individual tests only. I don't like group tests. The classroom was too cold every time!!
S13	Having a curriculum that works is very important to the achievement of students. I have a much better understanding of how far education has come over time. I actually tried group testing in my 4th grade classroom similar to Dr. Hanshaw's idea. I told my students we did it at Ole Miss and wanted their opinions on testing this way. After trying it, the students loved it. Even though I used the grade as a daily grade rather than a test grade, I witnessed great discussions within each team. Everyone participated on some level and they helped each other with writing the answers.

Table 4.1 Portfolio Comments of Teachers and Graduate Students (Continued)

Student	Comment
S14	The professor of this course, Dr. Hanshaw, wrote his dissertation on group involvement, specializing in group testing. I gained a lot of positive aspects from group testing and group involvement such as the use of long-term memory in discussing test information. I feel like I gained more from group testing because we discussed ideas out loud. Usually, I use my short-term memory when doing a test on my own. I was able to share with teachers of older students the method of group testing. Since I teach kindergarten, I can see the value of group work and allowing students to talk and learn from one another.
S15	Group and cooperative assessments were a new concept to me. Prior to this class, I had never participated in or saw the implementation of this form of assessment. It was important that my group members and I effectively communicated and cooperated both during and prior to assessment. Members worked to assure that fellow group members understood the content as well as acquiring clarity on concepts for themselves. Because of this need, my group members and I established e-mail communication to discuss areas of uncertainty. An atmosphere was established that aided in the discussion of the content studied. Also, a new mode of thinking was developed. My attention was no longer focused solely on my learning and achieving, but expanded to encompass the entire group. Although we were all provided with individual test papers, discussions evolved for each question; often providing new outlooks. I became more attentive to the views of the instructor as well as to those of peers. This transferred to my work. Through this expanded focus, I was better able to explore the avenue of curriculum theories and practices. With more in depth exploration, a greater knowledge-base was acquired and the content of my work improved.
S16	Cooperation skills in this class were addressed in the evaluation portion. Students were grouped together randomly and allowed to take group tests. This fostered cooperation because each member of the group was responsible for learning a certain portion of the material. The remainder of the group depended on each other to

Table 4.1 Portfolio Comments of Teachers and Graduate Students (Continued)

Student	Comment
	pull their own weight for an acceptable grade.
S17	Communication is this class was refined and enhanced in a different manner than I was used to. We were arranged by the professor into groups to take our tests. By working with classmates to talk out information learned, I was able to better my test score than if I had completed the test alone. Communication was also refined by class participation and discussion. I also learned that students tend to learn more if they have the ability to communicate to the teacher and to each other to enhance learning. Communication is not a one way street; both teacher and student need to communicate.

directly from the required portfolios of graduate students (i.e., some of whom are teachers). The designations S1, S2, etc., designate the students who wrote the remarks presented.

Closing Comments

In Chapter 1 of this book, several cooperative learning principles (Individual Responsibility and Face-to-face Interaction, Complex/Critical Thinking, Common Goal Orientation, and Extrinsic and Intrinsic Motivation) were presented as driving forces within the Cooperative Testing Environment Model presented in this book. These principles were promoted as strengthening factors operating within episodes of cooperative testing. The discussion of these factors and their relationship to both cooperative testing and learning was supported greatly by similar perspectives expressed in the work of Johnson and Johnson (1999), Slavin (1995), and Jacobs (2000).

A review of the remarks in Table 4.1 underscores not only what authors like those above have observed, but the above student experiences also confirm the importance of the four "spokes" depicted in Figure 1.1. Collectively, then, the portfolio comments of teachers and graduate students indicate the importance of the psychological and social components of cooperative efforts. Repeatedly, students mentioned such things as enjoying having less stress during testing, helping others and themselves succeed, and gaining new ways of thinking about learning. Ideas such as feeling a sense of responsibility to be prepared and knowing that success could be enhanced through group efforts (i.e., members were likely to pick up each other's slack) may have made efforts to collaborate a commonly shared goal appealing to all. Although important, making the highest grade was not the most commonly mentioned aspect of cooperative testing or learning found in the comments of this, admittedly, small sample of students. Nevertheless, the power of cooperative testing and learning, apparently, helps to create new friendships and new perspectives about the complexities of learning that go far beyond the obvious joys of students who may earn exceptional grades from cooperative learning and testing experiences. Therefore, I feel confident that very similar experiences and outcomes await others who might utilize cooperative learning and testing methodologies to enhance learning and achievement in K-12 and higher education classrooms alike.

Appendix

Table A.1 Alternative Cooperative Testing Arrangements

Author(s)/ (yr)	Cooperative Arrangement	Results/ Conclusion
Becker, R. (1995)	Open-book, open-notes group work, lab-practical final exam format used in highschool chemistry classes at semester's end. Students graded on separate curves for similar achieving homogeneous groups in different classes. Instructor used 30 questions for each laboratory final exam that lasted approximately 90 minutes.	Students realized that year-end exam demands good note taking and that such notes are valuable as a database even after the chemistry course ended. Additionally, students learned the value of working together, relying on each other's expertise on different parts of an assignment, and benefitting from the combined critical reviews of each other's work within a cooperative structure. Both students and other chemistry faculty liked the cooperative testing format.
Bonniface, D. (1985)	Students allowed to use notes and textbooks during an open-book examination. Students' amount of use of notes and the textbook were correlated with previous achievement in subject area as well as with test scores and a course questionnaire.	Fewer good grades were earned by students who spent the greatest amount of time using notes and the textbook. These students also had poor performance on previous course exams.

Table A.1 Alternative Cooperative Testing Arrangements (Continued)

Author(s)/ (yr)	Cooperative Arrangement	Results/ Conclusion
Eilertson and Valdermo (2000)	Authors examined effects of open-book testing on learning and instruction among 13 teachers and 350 secondary students in Norway.	Results indicated that understanding was improved in both cooperative and regular classrooms due to influence of open-book testing format.
Francis, J. (1982)	Authors explored the use of open-books during English literature examinations. Of interest was whether or not this format reduced anxiety and lessened the memorization of course material.	Students using open-books performed at a higher level, experienced less anxiety, and had less of a need to memorize course information than those who took a traditional test.
Ioannidou, M. (1997)	A comparison in achievement was made between 72 Cypress college students some of whom took open-book exams and while others took closed-book exams.	Although there was no significant difference between the total exam scores of the two formats, students taking the closed-book format had slightly higher scores.
Theophilides, C. and Koutselini, M. (2000)	Authors examined perceptions of students regarding how they studied prior to an examination and the way they performed during an examination in the open-book and closed-book formats. 181 students and their perceptions of the two formats was the focus of the study as measured by student ratings of 39 statements about study behavior.	Among the students who took the closed-book format, studying was postponed until just before the test. They also focused mostly on the assigned text and tended to memorize the course information. Students who took open-book examinations tended to engage the material more intensely, consulted other textbooks, worked creatively with and cross-related

Table A.1 Alternative Cooperative Testing Arrangements (Continued)

Author(s)/ (yr)	Cooperative Arrangement	Results/ Conclusion
		the acquired information. Students who took open-book tests had higher composite scores than students who took tests in the closed-book format. Differences in composite scores were statistically significant.
Weber, L. J. and McBee, J. K. (1993)	Authors investigated factors related to cheating on open-book, closed-book, and take-home examinations. Multiple choice tests and a statistical method that identified flagrant cheaters were used to determine the amount of cheating among the formats studied.	Investigators found that motivational factors may account for the amount of cheating on examinations and that both take-home and open-book exam takers produced no more evidence supporting cheating than those who took closed-book exams.
Weber, L. J., McBee, J. K, and Krebs, J. E. (1983)	Investigators examined differential effects on achievement on on knowledge questions and cognitive-skill items in three testing formats: closed-book, open-book, and take-home examinations. Student attitudes (anxiety), and items related to cheating were also explored.	Researchers found that cheating was not a problem. In the take-home format, knowledge item scores were higher and anxiety levels were lower.

Closing Comments

Readers from the 60's and 70's may have experienced, as I did, some form of the alternative cooperative testing arrangements discussed above. Arrangements where students utilize an outside source is arguably one where a form of cooperation exists between students and the assistance they receive from either notes and/or a textbook.

Although few in number, these examples highlight the open landscape of efforts still being employed to enhance student achievement and learning. In addition to cooperative testing and learning research, past and present, that may appear in journals and books, it is still most important to further research efforts that will take these and other methodologies into the regular classrooms of both K-12 and higher education teachers. I found the above accounts of participation in cooperative testing to be reflectively refreshing and, more so, stimulating reminders of why it is important to investigate which practices work and why they work for teachers and learners in the classrooms of schools at all levels.

References

Armstrong, D. G.,and T.V. Savage. 1990. *Secondary education: An introduction*. 2nd ed. New York: Macmillan.

———. 1998.*Teaching in the secondary school: An introduction*. 4th ed. Upper Saddle River, NJ: Prentice-Hall.

Becker, R. 1995. *Final analysis: Rethinking an age-old practice. Journal of Chemical Education* 72, no. 9 (September): 816-819.

Berry, J. J.,and W. M. Leonard, III. *Two heads are better than one?: Innovations in teaching sociology*. Presented in 'Innovations in Undergraduate Education' Section, annual meeting of the *American Sociological Association*, Montreal, Canada (August 25-29, 1974):1-8.

Boniface, D. 1985. *Candidates' use of notes and textbooks during an open-book examination.. Educational Research 27, no. 3 (November): 201-209*, http://0-web15.epnet.com.umiss.lib.olemiss.edu/DeliveryPrintSave.asp?tb=1&ug =sid+E5...(accessed August 18, 2004).

Bowen, C. W., and A. J. Phelps. 1997. Demonstration-based cooperative testing in general chemistry: *A broader assessment-of-learning technique. Journal of Chemical Education* 74, no. 6 (June): 715-719.

Brooks, J. G.,and M. G. Brooks. 1993. *In search of understanding: The case for the constructivist classroom*. Alexandria, VA: The Association for Supervision and Curriculum Development.

Bruning, J. L.,and B. L. Kintz. 1969. *Computational* handbook *of statistics*. 2nd ed. Glenview, IL: Scott, Foresman and Company.

———. *Computational handbook of statistics*. 1997. 4th ed. Reading, MA: Addison-Wesley Longman.

Cohen, J. 1988. *Statistical power analysis for the behavioral sciences*. 2nd ed. Hillsdale, NJ: Lawrence Erlbaum Associates.

Dougherty, R. C., C. W. Bowen, T. Berger, W. Rees, E. K. Mellon, and E. Pulliam. 1995. *Cooperative learning and enhanced communication: Effects on student performance, retention, and attitudes in general chemistry. Journal of Chemical Education* 72, no. 9 (September): 793, http://jchemed.chem. wisc.edu/journal/issues/1995/Sep/abs793.html (accessed October 14, 2005).

Eilertsen, T. V.,and Tor Valdermo. 2000. *Open-book assessment: A contribution to improved learning. Studies in Educational Evaluation* 26, no. 2: 91-103, http://0-web15.epnet.com.umiss.lib.olemiss.edu/citation.asp?tb=1&_ug =sid+E58ED1EF%...(accessed August 18, 2004).

References

Felder, R. 2001. *Active/cooperative learning: Best practices in engineering education.* Interview by Susan Ledlow, Clemson University, March 19, 2001, http://cite.asu.edu/active/feldertranscript.html (accessed November 11, 2003).

Felder, R.,and R. Brent. October, 1994. *Cooperative learning in technical courses: Procedures, pitfalls, and payoffs.* Work supported by National Science Foundation Division of Undergraduate Education Grant DUE-9354379, http:// www.ncu.edu/felder-public/Papers/Coopreport.html (accessed September 8, 2004).

Francis, J. 1982. *A case for open-book examinations. Educational Review* 34, no. 1 (February): 13-26, http://0-web15.epnet.com.umiss.lib.olemiss.edu/DeliveryPrintSave.asp?tb=1&_ug=sid+E5...(accessed August 18, 2004).

Furuhata, Y. 1965. *An experimental study of cooperation and competition: On group participation, group cohesiveness and group productivity. Japanese Journal of Educational Psychology 13, no. 4:1-13, http://web32.epnet.com.umiss.lib.olemiss.edu/DeliveryPrintSave.asp?tb=1&_ug=sid+96...(accessed October 5, 2005).

Green, S. B., N. J. Salkind, and T. M. Akey. 2000. *Using spss for windows: Analyzing and understanding data.* 2nd ed. Upper Saddle River, NJ: Prentice-Hall.

Hall, R. H., M. A. SidioHall, and C. B. Saling.. *A comparison of learning strategies within the context of a post-secondary class: Effects on initial learning and transfer.* Presentation at the annual meeting of the *American Educational Research Association*, New York, NY (April, 1996): 1of 3, http://medialab.umr.edu/rhall/research_coop_learning.shtml (accessed November 12, 2003).

Hall, R. H., B. M. Mancini, J. L. Hall. August, 1996. *Scripted cooperative learning and testing in a post-secondary class.* Presentation at the annual meeting of the *American Psychological Association*, Toronto, Canada (August, 1996):1of 3, http://medialab.umr.edu/rhall/research_coop_learning.shtml (accessed November 12, 2003).

Hancock, D. *Cooperative learning and peer orientation effects on motivation. Journal of Educational Research* 97, no. 3: 159-165.

Hanshaw, L. G. 1976. *Test anxiety, self-concept, and the test performance of students paired for testing and the same students working alone.* Ph.D. diss., University of Southern Mississippi.

———. 1982. *Test anxiety, self-concept, and the test performance of students paired for testing and the same students working alone. Science Education* 66, no. 1: 15-24.

Hodges, J. C. May, 1996. *The effects of cooperative learning on performance and attitude toward learning in high school biology.* Educational specialist thesis, University of Mississippi.

Husband, R. W. Fall, 1940. *Cooperative versus solitary problem solution. The*

Journal of Social Psychology 11: 405-409.

Ioannidou, M. K. 1997. *Testing and life-long learning: Open-book and closed-book examination in a university course.* Studies in Educational Evaluation 23, no. 2: 131-139, http://0-web15.epnet.com.umiss.lib.olemiss.edu/DeliveryPrintSave.asp?tb=1&_ug=sid+E5... (accessed August 18, 2004).

Jacobs, G. M. 2000. *Cooperative learning in the thinking classroom: Research and theoretical perspectives.* http://www.geocities.com/Athens/Thebes/1650/coopthk.html (accessed October 15, 2000).

Johnson, D. W., and R. T. Johnson. 1999. Learning together and alone: Co-operative, competitive, and individualistic learning, 5th ed. Needham, MA: Allyn and Bacon.

Johnson, D. W., R. T. Johnson, E. Holubec, and P. Roy. 1984. *Circles of learning.* Alexandria, VA: Association for Supervision and Curriculum Development.

Johnson, R. T., and D. W. Johnson. 1994. *An overview of cooperative learning. In Creativity and Collaborative Learning,* ed. J. Thousand, A. Villa, and A. Nevin, (Baltimore: Brookes Press, 1994). http://www.cooplearn.org/pages/overviewpaper.html (accessed September 8, 2004).

Johnson, D. W., R. Johnson, and K. A. Smith. 1991. *Active learning: Cooperation in the college classroom.* Edina, MN: Interaction Book Company.

Kauchak, D., and P. Eggen. 2005. *Introduction to teaching: Becoming a professional,* 2nd ed. Upper Saddle River, NJ: Pearson Prentice-Hall.

Kaufman, D. B., R. M. Felder, and H. Fuller. 2000. *Accounting for individual effort in cooperative learning teams. Journal of Engineering Education* 89, no. 2:133-140.

Lambiotte, J. G., D. F. Dansereau, T. R. Rocklin, B. Fletcher, V. I. Hythecker, C. O. Larson, and A. M. O'Donnell. 1987. *Cooperative learning and test taking: Transfer of skills. Contemporary Educational Psychology* 12, no. 1: 52-61, http://0-web22.epnet.com.umiss.lib.olemiss.edu/citation.asp?tb=1&_ug=sid+C4A9F3A8%... (accessed September 30, 2005).

Ledlow, S. 1999. *Group grades in cooperative learning classes.* Arizona State University: Instructional Innovation Network. http://www.public.asu.edu/~ledlow/sledlow/group.html (accessed August 26, 2005).

Lindquist, E. F. 1953. Design and analysis of experiments in psychology and education. Cambridge, MA: Houghton-Mifflin Company.

McKeachie, W. J. 1988. *Teaching thinking. In National Center for Research for the Improvement of Postsecondary Teaching and Learning Update* 1, no. 2: 81.

Meinster, M. O., and K. C. Rose. 1993. *Cooperative testing in introductory-level psychology courses. Teaching of psychology: Ideas and innovations.* Proceedings of the 7th annual conference on Undergraduate Teaching of Psychology, Ellenville, NY.

References

Monk-Turner, E., and B. Payne. Spring, 2005. *Addressing issues in group work in the classroom.* Journal of Criminal Justice Education 16, Issue 1: 166-179, http://0-web22.epnet.com.umiss.lib.olemiss.edu/DeliveryPrintSave.asp?tb=1&_ug=sid+C4... (accessed September 30, 2005).

Orbell, J. M., A. J. Van de Kragt, and R. M. Dawes. 1988. *Explaining discussion-induced cooperation.* Journal of Personality & Social Psychology 54, no. 5: 811-819, http://0-web32.epnet.com.umiss.lib.olemiss.edu/citation.asp?tb=1&_ug=sid+96E5F2EF%2... (accessed October 5, 2005).

Piaget, J. 1980. *Experiments in contradiction.* Chicago: University of Chicago Press.

Pintrich, P. R. 1990. *Implications of psychological research on student learning and college teaching for teacher education. In Handbook of Research on Teacher Education,* ed. W. R. Houston (New York: Macmillan, 1990).

Reid, J. B., R. L. Palmer, J. Whitlock, and J. Jones. August, 1973. *Computer-assisted instruction performance of student pairs as related to individual differences.* The Journal of Educational Psychology 65: 65-73.

Ruggiero, V. R. 1988. *Teaching thinking across the curriculum.* New York: Harper and Row.

Salkind, N. J. 2000. *Statistics for people who (think they) hate statistics.* Sage Publications, Inc.

Skidmore, R. L., L. Aagaard. 2004. *The relationship between testing condition and student test scores.* Journal of Instructional Psychology 31, no. 4: 304-313, http//0-web32.epnet.com.umiss.lib.olemiss.edu/citation.asp?tb=1&_ug=sid+233C234B%2...(accessed September 30, 2005).

Slavin, R. E. 1995. *Coopeartive learning: Theory, research, and practice.* 2nd ed. Needham Heights, MA: Allyn and Bacon.

Smith, K., A., and A. A. Waller. 2004. *Cooperative learning for new college teachers.* http://aral.cps.msu.edu/CPS101FS97/CPS101Staff/CommonToAllTracks/CoopLearning.html (accessed September 8, 2004).

Springer, L., M. E. Stanne, and S. Donovan. November, 1997. *Measuring the success of small-group learniing in college-level SMET teaching: A meta-analysis.* Madison, WI: National Institute for Science Education Wisconsin Center for Education Research. http://www.wcer.wisc.edu/nise/CL1/CL/resource/scismet.html (accessed November 11, 2003).

Steinbrink, J. E., and R. M. Jones. 1993. *Coopeartive test-review tea student achievement.* Clearing House 66, no. 5: 307-311, http://0-web22.epnet.com.umiss.lib.olemiss.edu/citation.asp?tb=1&_ug=sid+C4A9F3A8%...(accessed September 30, 2005).

Sutter, E. G., and J. B. Reid. 1969. *Learner variables and interpersonal conditions in computer-assisted instruction.* The Journal of Educational Psychology 60: 153-157.

Taylor, D. W., and W. L. Faust. December, 1952. *Twenty questions: Efficiency in problem solving as a function of size of group.* The Journal of

References

Experimental Psychology 44: 360-368.
Theophilides, C., and M. Koutselini. 2000. *Study behavior in the closed-book and the open-book examination: A comparative analysis. Educational Research and Evaluation* 6, no. 4: 379-393.
Thorndike, R. M., and D. L. Dinnel. 2001. *Basic statistics for the behavioral sciences.* Upper Saddle River, NJ: Prentice-Hall.
Tien, L. T., V. Roth, and J. A. Kampmeier. 2002. *Implementation of a peer-led team learning instructional approach in an undergraduate organic chemistry course. Journal of Research in Science Teaching* 39, Issue 7: 602-632, http://www3.interscience.wiley.com/cgi-bin/abstract/97518099/ABSTRACT (accessed October 14, 2005).
Vygotsky, L. 1978. Mind in society: The development of higher mental processes. Cambridge, MA: Harvard University Press.
Webb, N. M. 1997. *Assessing students in small cooperative groups. Theory Into Practice* 36, no. 4: 205-213.
Weber, L. J., J. K. McBee, and J. E. Krebs. 1983. *Take-home tests: An experimental study. Research in Higher Education* 18, no. 4: 473-483, http://0-web15.epnet..com.umiss.lib.olemiss.eduDeliveryPrintSave.asp?tb=1&_ug=sid+E5... (accessed August 18, 2004).
Weber. L. J., J. K. McBee. 1983. *Cheating: A problem with take-home exams?* Paper presented at the annual meeting of the *National Council on Measurement in Education* (Montreal, Canada, April 11-15, 1983), http://web15.epnet.com.umiss.lib.olemiss.edu/DeliveryPrintSave.asp?tb=1&_ug=sid+E5... (accessed August 18, 2004).
Weinberg, A., F. Fischer, and H. Mandl. 2002. *Fostering individual transfer and knowledge convergence in text-based computer-mediated communication.* Ludwig-Maximilians-University of Munich: Institute of Educational Psychology. http://newmedia.colorado.edu/cscl/153.html (accessed October 5, 2005).
Wertsh, J. V. 1991. *Voices of the mind: A sociocultural approach to mediated action.* Cambridge, MA: Harvard University Press.
Williams, R. L., E. Carroll, and B. Hautau. September, 2005. *Individual accountability in cooperative learning groups at the college level: Differential effects on high, average, and low exam performers. Journal of Behavioral Education* 14, Issue 3: 167-188, http://0-web22.epnet.com.umiss.lib.Olemiss.edu/citation.asp?tb=1&_ug=sid+C4A9F3A8%... (accessed September 30, 2005).
Wittrock, M. C. 1974. *Learning as a generative process. Educational Psychologist* 11: 87-95.
Woolfolk, A. E. 1998. Educational psychology. 7th ed. Needham Heights, MA: Allyn and Bacon.
Zimbardo, P. G., L. D. Butler, and V. A. Wolfe. Winter, 2003. *Cooperative college examinations: More gain, less pain when students share informa-*

tion and grades. Journal of Experimental Education 71, no. 2: 101-125, http://0-web2.epnet.com.umiss.lib.olemiss.edu/citation.asp?tb=1&_ug=sid+7DBB77DE%... (accessed August 18, 2004).

Index

Aagaard, Lola, 17, 27
Absenteeism, of group mates, 5
Accountability of students
   in cooperative testing groups, 4-5, 29; in cooperative testing model, 4-5
Achievement
   cooperative learning and, 2, 2fig.1.1, 3, 7-9; cooperative testing and, 2, 2fig.1.1, 3, 11table1.1, 33
Akey, Theresa M., 40-41
Altruism, and cooperative learning, 54
Armstrong, David G., 3, 5, 6
Becker, Robert, 61
Berger, T., 11
Berry, James J., 11
Bowen, Craig W., 11
Boniface, D., 61
Brent, Rebecca, 9, 12, 22
Brooks, Jacqueline G., 28
Brooks, Martin G., 28
Bruning, James L., 39
Butler, Lisa D., 9, 21, 24
Carroll, Erin, 20
Cohen, Jacob, 40
Continuum
   instruction, reinforcement, and evaluation, 1, 23, 23fig.2.1, 24
Cooperative learning, 1;
   achievement and, 2, 2fig.1.1, 3, 7-9; alternative approaches to, 24 altruism and, 54; cognitive development and, 7; definition of, 1, 7; different approaches to using, 24-25; factors; 3, 7-9; goal of, 7; group success, 4; paired-cooperative condition and, 1; motivation and, 2, 2fig,1.1, 3-4, 6-7, 24; research findings, 3, 7-9; strengthening factors, 2fig.1.1; student accountability and, 2, 4-5; within cooperative testing environment, 1, 3, 7
Cooperative testing environment model, 25-33; applications in science classrooms, 51; student-role in, 26fig.2.2; 34-35; teacher-selected method and, 26fig.2.2, 27-28; teacher-role and, 26fig.2.2, 29-32
Cooperative testing, 1, 7-9;
   common goal orientation and, 2fig.1.1, 4, 6; comparison of means and, 35-39; complex/critical thinking and, 2, 5, 9; correlational statistics and, 40; definition of, 1; extrinsic motivation and, 2, 6-7; face-to-face interaction and, 2, 5; four spokes and, 4; group success and, 4; individual accountability and, 2fig.1.1, 4-5, 29; individual responsibility and, 2fig.1.1, 4; intrinsic motivation and, 2fig.1.1, 6-7; psychology supporting, 2fig,1.1, qualitative considerations and, 53-64; research and, 10-22; science classes and, 51-52; strengthening factors and, 2fig.1.1

Dansereau, Donald F., 14
Dawes, Robin M., 16
Dinnel, Dale L., 40
Donovan, Samuel, 17, 25
Dougherty, R. C., 11
Effect size estimates, 36-48table3.1
  Eta^2 and, 39-41; median view of, 40-41; Wilks' Lambda (λ) and, 39-40
Eggen, Paul, 5, 7
Eilertson, Tor V., 62
Faust, William L., 18
Felder, Richard M., 9, 12, 14, 19, 22, 27
Fischer, Frank, 20
Fletcher, Bennett, 14
Francis, John, 62
Fuller, Hugh, 14
Furuhata, Yasuyoshi, 12
Goals
  group goals, 4, 34, 41
Gold brick effect, 4
  cooperative learning and, 4, 31; cooperative testing and, 4
Grading
  individual answers and, 39; common answers and, 41
Group interactions, 1, 7;
  expectations and, 4, 28
Green, Samuel B., 39, 40
Hall, J. L., 13
Hall, Richard M., 12-13
Hancock, Dawson, 13
Hanshaw, Larry G., 1, 9, 13, 27, 31, 39, 51
Hauta, Briana, 20
Hodges, Janet C., 51-52
Holubec, E., 3
Husband, Richard, 14
Hythecker, V. I., 14
Intra-group position changes, 41-48;
  method of calculating values and,
49-50; prediction equation from, 49; subgroups and, 42
Ioannidou, Mary K., 62
Jacobs, George M., 5, 8-9, 25, 58
Johnson, David W., 1, 3, 5, 8, 27, 30, 33, 35, 60
Johnson, Roger T., 1, 3, 5, 8, 25, 28, 31, 33, 58
Jones, Jean, 16
Jones, Robert M., 25, 29
Kampmeier, J. A., 19
Kauchak, Donald, 5, 7
Kaufman, Deborah B., 14
Kintz, B. L., 39
Koutselini, Mary, 62
Krebs, J. E., 63
Lambiotte, Judith G., 14, 29
Larson, C. O., 14
Ledlow, Susan, 1, 4, 15
Leonard, Wilbert M., III, 11
Lindquist, Edward F., 41
Mancini, B. M., 13
Mandl, Heinz, 20
Mellon, E. K., 11
McBee, Janice K., 63
McKeachie, Wilbert J., 5
Meinster, Martha O., 9, 15, 25, 28-29, 31, 41
Monk-Turner, Elizabeth, 15, 31
Motivation, 2, 6-7
  cooperative learning and, 6-7
  extrinsic rewards and, 2, 6-7
  intrinsic rewards, 2, 6-7
O'Donnell, A. M., 14
Orbell, John M., 16, 25, 29
Palmer, Richard L., 16
Payne, Brian, 15, 31
Phelps, Amy J., 11
Piaget, Jean, 5;
  complex thinking and, 5

Pintrich, Paul R., 5
Portfolio comments, 53-59;
   graduate students and, 54-58;
   teachers and, 54-58
Pulliam, E., 11
Rees, W., 11
Reid, Jackson B., 16, 18
Rewards, 2, 6-7
   cooperative learning and, 2fig.1.1;
   extrinsic rewards and, 2, 2fig.1.1, 6-7
   group rewards and, 4
   intrinsic rewards and, 2, 2fig.1.1, 6-7
   motivation and, 2, 6-7, 33, 39
Rocklin, Thomas R., 14
Rose, Karen C., 9, 15, 25, 28-29, 31, 41
Roth, Vicki, 19
Roy, P., 3
Ruggiero, Vincent R., 5
Saling, C. B., 12
Salkind, Neil J., 39-40, 49
Savage, Tom V., 3, 5, 6, 9
Science teacher's specialist field study, 51-52
Sidio-Hall, M. A., 12
Skidmore, Ronald L., 17, 27
Slavin, Robert E., 3, 5, 8, 25, 31, 33, 50, 58
Smith, Karl A., 4, 25
Springer, Leonard, 17, 25
Stanne, Mary E., 18, 25
Steinbrink, John E., 25, 29
Sutter, Emily G., 18
Taylor, Donald W., 18
Theophilides, Christos, 62
Thorndike, Robert M., 40
Tien, Lydia T., 19
Valdermo, Odd, 62
Van de Kragt, Alphons J., 16
Vygotsky, Lev, 1, 24-25
Waller, A. A., 4, 25
Webb, Noreen M., 1, 24, 41

Weber, Larry J., 63
Weinberger, Armin, 20
Wertsh, James V., 25
Whitlock, J., 16
Wilks' Lambda, 39-40
Williams, Robert L., 20
Wittrock, A. E., 5, 9
Wolfe, Valerie A., 9, 21, 24
Woolfolk, Anita E., v, 1, 32
Zimbardo, Philip G., 9, 21, 24, 25, 41